THE WORTHY MIND

TRANSFORM Your Mindset.

STRENGTHEN Self-Worth.

MEADOW DeVOR

 sourcebooks

Published by Sourcebooks
P.O. Box 4410, Naperville, Illinois 60567-4410
(630) 961-3900
sourcebooks.com

Originally published as *The Worthy Project* in 2021 in the United
States by Audible Originals, an imprint of Audible, Inc.

Cataloging-in-Publication Data is on file with the Library of Congress.

Printed and bound in the United States of America.
SB 10 9 8 7 6 5 4 3 2 1

Contents

Introduction

If you've opened this book, it's probably because you feel like your life doesn't quite fit. You rarely feel seen or understood. You don't know what makes you happy. You might be experiencing a painful emptiness, and you don't know how to fill it. Or you struggle with frustration, resentment, overwhelm, and a deep fear that you aren't good enough, pretty enough, smart enough, or *worthy* enough to live a genuinely good life.

I can assure you you're not alone and that there's something better awaiting you. Having spent almost twenty years as a coach, author, and personal development teacher, I've worked with countless students navigating these issues, and I've struggled with them myself. And I can tell you that to step into your own worth, you first have to understand the root cause of unworthiness, and it's this: No matter who you are, what you've done, where you've come from, or what you've overcome, there's an important part of you that's been lost. Let's call her *the lost self*. She's the part of you that you've denied, pushed away, repressed, controlled, or silenced.

She holds all your discarded pieces, the qualities that you didn't want to keep—things that were too threatening, too dangerous, or too confusing for you to carry. There was no other choice. You had to push those pieces away. This was the only way to save yourself. At some point, you learned that those parts of you were a threat—maybe to your mom, your sister, your dad, a teacher, a friend, a boss, or a lover. And you didn't want to be a threat. So you learned who you were supposed to be, and you tried to become it.

Your mind knew the rules. You weren't supposed to be angry. You weren't supposed to be sensitive. You couldn't be selfish. You shouldn't take up too much space. You learned that you had to be less of you and more of what someone else wanted.

So you made yourself friendlier. And you made your voice sweeter. And you made sure to always think about others first. You volunteered for things you didn't want to do. You forgot how to say no. You made yourself smaller.

Or at least you tried.

To get your vital needs met—connection, security, sustenance, belonging, love—your mind learned to cut off pieces of yourself and tuck them far away. And the more secrets your mind buried, the more you lost yourself.

> **When you're living as a fraction of who you really are, you only experience a fraction of what you're worth.**

And this affects everything, and I do mean *everything*. The quality of your relationships, your career, your home life, your emotional health—it all comes down to one thing. This one thing? An unwavering understanding of your own immeasurable value. This understanding is at the core of how you see yourself and how you allow the world to see you. It is what I call "worth."

Self-worth, worthy, worthiness... These words are tricky because you know that you're supposed to value yourself, but what does it actually mean to cultivate self-worth, and how do you do it?

Worthiness is the quality of deserving attention, energy, and respect. Throughout this book, I'll share practical guidelines and action steps that can be put into practice immediately—what I call "worthy work." These action steps will teach you how to feel, act, and live as if you are worthy.

Worthy work is brave work. To live with the fullest expression of your intrinsic worth, you must learn to embrace every part of you. And that's not easy. It takes courage, compassion, and a lot of practice. In this book, you're not going to learn how to be a better, smarter, more polished version of you. Nor are you going to learn how to have better habits, how to improve your image, or how to make people like you.

> **Because worthiness isn't about making yourself into a better version of you. It's about unapologetically owning who you are, in all your magnificence and all your messiness. Right here. Right now. It's about reclaiming, integrating, and celebrating what's been lost so that you can embrace the complicated brilliance of who you really are.**

By recovering what's been lost, you gain full access to your worthy mind, a mind that has an unwavering understanding of your immeasurable value. A mind that no longer hides parts of you, a mind that embraces all of you. A mind that revels in the brightness of you without the need to protect, defend, or hide your light. A mind that compassionately honors even the darkest of flaws without the need to criticize, chastise, or condemn.

In my work, I've been able to develop tools for strengthening self-worth. This experience has profoundly changed my understanding of who I am, what I am worth, and how I live my life. My job is to share these tools with you so that you can feel, act, and live with an unwavering and abiding sense of worthiness. I've done this work myself, and I've taught thousands of others to do the same. I'll share some of my personal stories as well as those of my students throughout this book.

In my previous book, *The Worthy Project*, I taught how to stop undervaluing yourself, how to stop giving yourself away for cheap, and how to start investing in yourself. I showed how you can consciously change your behavior so that you can reinforce your sense of self-worth. Thanks to the success of *The Worthy Project*, I've been asked to take this work to the next level. Where *The Worthy Project* focused on how behavior affects self-worth, *The Worthy Mind* focuses on the conscious and unconscious beliefs that influence your self-worth.

In this book, you'll learn a counterintuitive and powerful way to transform how you think about yourself. First, you'll find out why you lost yourself in the first place. You'll discover the mechanisms behind how the mind fractured to conceal the truth. You'll find out exactly what was lost and what took its place. You'll see what happens when your lost self stays hidden and the enormous toll it takes on your sense of self-worth. Then, you'll learn how to reclaim, restore, and reintegrate what's been lost so you can treasure, cherish, and care for your lost self. Finally, you'll learn to rely on the wisdom of your worthy mind so you can live with a rock-solid understanding of your infinite worth. And throughout the book, you'll be given unexpected, actionable steps to help you put these concepts to work right away.

LET'S GET STARTED

Take a moment to think about how you show up in your life, right here, right now. Think about what you're willing to expose, with whom you're willing to share, and what you might try to hide or conceal. Maybe you feel safest being yourself among strangers because you don't have to live up to preconceived notions, or maybe you only share yourself with your closest confidants because you've been hurt in the past. Think about what you've silenced in yourself, what you've rejected about yourself, what you've learned to repress and deny—the angry parts, the sad parts, the shameful parts. Maybe you do your best to portray yourself as perky and positive, or maybe you go out of your way to avoid others because you feel like you'll never measure up. Think about the parts of you that you hide—the impolite parts, the strong parts, the fierce parts. Maybe you don't share an important achievement because you've been ridiculed for doing so in the past. Maybe you censor your conversations because you're afraid you'll be ostracized or exiled from your workplace, your church, or your friend group. Think about how much thought, energy, and effort you have spent trying to create a tolerable, likable, good enough you. These actions—trying to be what others want, worrying about what others feel, working to meet other people's needs, and shape-shifting yourself to conform to what others believe—are all symptoms of the same underlying problem: You have lost crucial pieces of yourself. You've lost access to what you want, what you feel, what you need, and what you believe, and your self-worth has taken a hit.

Now imagine who you were before you lost yourself. Picture that little you, the one who hadn't been denied, pushed away, repressed, controlled, or silenced yet. Even if you can't remember her, she still lives inside you. Imagine how different your life would be today if she'd been taught that she was allowed to be angry, scared, or sad. Maybe you'd be willing to be more vulnerable in your relationships, or you wouldn't feel guilty when you want to say no, or maybe you'd feel less pressure to perform and more freedom to make mistakes. Imagine if your lost self had been taught that she should take up as much space as she wants, speak her truth without censoring, and take more risks. Maybe today you'd feel more empowered to protect your boundaries, more willing to honor what your soul desires, and freer to feel uninhibited joy. Imagine if your lost self was never told that she should be different, smaller, or less visible. Maybe today you'd feel more courageous in your creative pursuits or more able to appreciate the miracle of your body, or maybe you'd be braver in social situations. Imagine what life would be like today if that sweet, innocent you had never been criticized, judged, or condemned. If instead, every aspect—good, bad, ugly, beautiful—had been supported, nurtured, and celebrated. Imagine what life would be like right now if you could liberate that beautiful, wild little you.

That wild little you, the self you lost, has always had access to your worthy mind. Your lost self holds important keys to your self-worth. By asking her questions, you can begin to unlock her secrets. So right up front, I am going to teach you how to start accessing your worthy mind. This technique can be used in line at the coffee shop, late at night before you go to bed, or outside on your favorite hiking trail. Rather than being distracted by those around you, this technique helps bring the spotlight back to you—an imperative component for building self-worth. It only takes a few seconds to learn, and it can radically change your life. Here it is: Take a moment, and imagine having a conversation with your lost self. Close your eyes, picture her in your mind, and take the time to really listen for the answers that arise from within you. Ask her these questions:

- *Who are you?*
- *What do you feel?*
- *What do you need?*
- *What do you love?*
- *What do you really want?*

Her answers often start with "I am... I feel... I need... I love... I really want..." In practice, it might sound like *"I am a mom. I feel angry. I need time alone. I love turquoise jewelry. I really want to feel safe."* Or it might sound like *"I am in a rut. I feel boxed in. I need adventure. I love the water. I really want to go to Mexico."* Or it might sound like *"I am tired. I feel lonely. I need to be touched. I love my dog. I really want a best friend."* No matter who you are, where you are, or how often you do it, this technique always works. How it works and what to do with this information are what you'll learn through the course of this book. I'll give you a preview: worthiness isn't shaped by the answers themselves.

> **Rather, worthiness is strengthened through the process of uncovering truths about who you are, what you feel, what you want, what you need, and what you love and then by taking action to own and celebrate these truths.**

By reclaiming what's been lost, you'll finally be free to live the fullest expression of your infinite worth.

Life wants all of you. It wants you to gather all your knowledge, all your gifts, all your weaknesses, and all your strengths. It wants you to bring this to every relationship, every room, every conversation, and every endeavor. It wants you to be brave. To be able to bring your entire self and to move through the world with a sense of purpose and full of ease—this is freedom. This is worthiness.

CHAPTER 1

Why You Lost Yourself

It's easy to miss an encounter with your lost self. By definition, the lost self isn't really a thing that you experience but more the absence of a thing. It's the hole that's left behind when you remove a piece of the puzzle. It's the blank space on the wall where there once hung a portrait. It's the silence, not the song. In hindsight, I can point to several places on the map of my life and say, right there, I came up against my lost self. And at those points, I may have even witnessed the shadow on the wall, but I wasn't ready to figure out what was casting it. Personal development work often comes down to a matter of triage. You deal with the thing that hurts the most. And then you deal with the next. For this reason, in the wake of a violent and turbulent childhood, I spent a few decades stitching myself back together before I was strong enough to tackle my crippling sense of worthlessness. And then, only after many years of researching and developing tools for building self-worth, did I begin to realize the importance of the lost self. And that particular journey began over a Thanksgiving weekend in a fancy hotel room in San Francisco.

It was two in the morning, and the hotel room was pitch-black. For as long as I could remember, nights had been long. Anxiety held itself at bay during the day, but in the early morning hours, it would seep in like a black fog and consume me. I'd wake up, heart pounding, as if I'd been running for my life. My daughter, Isabelle, was fourteen in real life, but in my dreams, she was always a toddler, and the dream was always the same: We were trapped in my childhood bedroom, and I was desperate to save her, to save us. I'd try to yell for help but wouldn't be able to make a sound. I'd try to run, but my legs would be too heavy to move. And then I'd wake up, gasping for breath.

There in the hotel, in the dense blackout curtain darkness, I didn't need to go anywhere to make sure she was safe. I lay still and listened for her breath. I could feel the warmth of her hand close to my cheek. She was my anchor back to adulthood, back to life with my daughter.

But the panic continued to thrum through my body. I heard something, maybe my own heartbeat, droning in my ears. *Thump, thump, thump, thump.* I stopped breathing, and the rumble got louder, closer. It was the sound of heavy footsteps muffled by carpet.

Every inch of my body stiffened. White-hot electricity jolted through me, alert, ready. The bedside lamp rumbled in rhythm as the footsteps approached. I grabbed my phone and turned on the flashlight. I needed light. I needed to remember where I was in time. I needed to remember that we weren't in my childhood home, that we weren't in danger. I needed to remember that nothing was wrong.

Someone paused right outside the door. I heard the sound of paper sliding against wood and carpet, the slip of something under the door. I waited until the steps retreated and then shone my light on the floor to see an envelope. It was the guest folio. We were due to check out in the morning.

Even though there was no obvious reason to be afraid, I couldn't calm my breathing. I tried to tell myself that nothing bad was happening, that we were safe. I tried to tell myself that I'd just heard the footsteps of a hotel worker, no big deal. Yet my body refused to believe me. A specific and unexplainable terror flooded through me, one that made no sense. I was physically overcome with a singular idea: my mother was coming to hurt us. Mind you, she had been dead for twenty years. So it wasn't that I thought my literal mother was coming down the hall. And it wasn't that my nightmare had suddenly come to life as some sort of PTSD flashback. I knew she was quite dead. But the terror was real, and it felt related to my mom in an almost supernatural way. I simultaneously had the distinct feeling of impending doom, like I was going to be punished, and the awareness that this feeling couldn't be true. My dead mother couldn't come after us, yet the feeling persisted.

Someone, somewhere was going to try to hurt us; somehow we were going to be abandoned.

This feeling that I had done something that deserved punishment, this wasn't the first time I'd felt like this. I tried to talk myself through it. "You're just having a trauma reaction. You'll get your bearings. You'll be okay." And yet there was a part of me over which I had no control. A part of me that refused to calm down. That part was wide awake and watching, listening, waiting for the inevitable hammer to fall.

Thanksgiving weekend at the Palace was a tradition for me and Isabelle. We'd go to a show. We'd go ice skating at Union Square. We'd order room service, and she'd order extra tiny ketchup bottles for her fries. We would wear fancy clothes and take a taxi to the theater. We had looked forward to this trip all year, yet lying there in the middle of the night, I felt like I needed to explain myself. *I am a grown woman. It's my own money. I'm hurting no one. I'm allowed to spend it how I want to spend it.*

No matter how much I tried to justify our trip, no matter how much I tried to assure myself that I had every right to be there with my daughter, to celebrate the holiday in the way I wanted, to spend my money in the way I wanted, I couldn't shake the feeling that I'd made a terrible mistake. I felt a crushing sense of guilt, and the evidence lay just inside my hotel door, inside that envelope. As if the folio itself held a detailed account of exactly how unworthy I was, exactly how selfish I'd been, exactly how much punishment I deserved. It felt as if the envelope itself held the sentence of abandonment and exile. I didn't want to look at it, so I turned my flashlight off and then immediately clicked it back on. The darkness felt too consuming, too dangerous.

I don't do well with chaos, and I tend to lean hard into hypervigilance when faced with feeling out of control. So to cope with this uncontrollable sense of consuming terror, I began charting the history of this feeling. When had I felt it? Why had I felt it? What was this thing that had seeped into my hotel room? I remembered having a similar reaction the night after I bought myself a sofa that I'd really wanted for my living room. I'd had this feeling when I'd purchased my beautiful ebony grand piano that now sat next to the new couch. I tried to figure out what it was. Was it anytime I'd spent money? No. I didn't feel it when I'd purchased the armoire for Isabelle's bedroom. I didn't feel it when I bought groceries. I didn't feel it when I paid the electric bill.

Seemingly unrelated memories surfaced in my mind. I remembered being small, eight, maybe nine years old. My jewelry box, with its emerald-green velvet interior and stained glass hummingbird on its lid, lay hidden under my bed. It contained a ring, a box of candy, and all the money I owned. I had stolen the ring from our local dime store. I'd fallen in love with that Minnie Mouse ring displayed next to the cash register and jettisoned myself into life as an outlaw before realizing that I'd never be able to explain how I'd come to own said ring. I remembered how I'd take it out of its hiding place so that I could look at it. It was beautiful and dainty, but I never dared to wear it. I knew the only way to keep it was to keep it hidden.

I remembered the candy, a partially eaten box of jujubes, chosen not because I liked them but because the pieces were small, and if I had one per day, I could make the box last for months. They tasted like petrified pieces of plastic, nearly inedible, but they were a private source of pride for me. I remembered how my sister would choose a candy that she loved and devour it within minutes. I, on the other hand, had chosen something that I didn't even like and then allowed myself as little of it as possible.

Inside the jujube box, I also kept a small roll of cash, eleven one-dollar bills. I felt about money the way I felt about candy. It was hard to come by and something to be carefully rationed. I don't remember how I'd gotten the money, other than it was through legitimate means, unlike the ring. Birthdays, Easters, Christmases, they all added up. And I don't remember what prompted my urge to finally spend the money, but I do remember what I bought. And God, I remembered wanting a Barbie more than I wanted to breathe. But I did not buy a Barbie. Instead, I bought a gift for my mom. The Barbie was just under ten dollars. I could afford it, but I was too scared to buy it.

Thinking about that Barbie gave me the same feeling that haunted me in the hotel room, the feeling of impending doom, that feeling that I would be punished. The feelings that I'd be abandoned. I remember knowing that I wouldn't be allowed to keep the Barbie. If I bought it, it'd be used against me—evidence that I was selfish and bad. So instead, I went to the kitchen aisle at the store and chose a ceramic container for wooden spoons—white stoneware with a chocolate-brown glazed rim. It would be a gift for my mother, and that was worth my entire wad of cash. Visible proof that I was worthy of my mom's love. That container stayed on her stove top until the day she died.

I lay in that hotel bed trying to make sense of it all. Though I didn't know it yet, I was closing in on my lost self. My memories were pointing toward what had been forgotten, painting a rudimentary picture, like the chalk outline of a body at a crime scene. Who I was, what I felt, what I needed, what I loved—those ideas weren't the most prominent aspects of my memories. Instead, there was evidence of things I loved but didn't allow myself. Things I wanted but couldn't have. Things I felt but denied. Those were shadows on the wall, but the one casting the shadows was simply a little girl. A little girl who'd stolen a ring because no one was going to get it for her otherwise. The little girl who'd rationed her shitty candy because she desperately needed something to look forward to. The little girl who'd wanted a Barbie, yes, but wanted to avoid corporal punishment even more.

Hidden inside the panic-stricken woman I had become, there was a little girl who I'd completely forgotten, and she had never left my side. She simply wanted permission to enjoy what was rightfully hers, with a promise that she wouldn't be punished for it. She wanted a mountain of candy and glamorous rings on all her fingers. She wanted to buy a Barbie for every little girl in San Francisco. She wanted to be allowed to own, experience, and feel worthy of what was rightfully hers. I'd lost her because it had been too dangerous to keep her. I'd forgotten her because it had been too painful to remember her. Now, she was the one I needed to protect, the one I needed to love, the one I needed to reclaim.

A BRILLIANT COPING MECHANISM

The lost self lives in the realm of what psychologist Carl Jung called the *shadow*. The shadow is the unknown or unconscious side of your personality.

The lost self becomes relegated to the shadow as a brilliant coping mechanism meant to shelter you from suffering, harm, and exile.

Even if you had the most spectacular upbringing, at some point, the answers to the questions *Who are you? What do you feel? What do you need? What do you love? What do you really want?* became threatening. Whether or not it was conscious, you learned that something was unacceptable or painful about your answers. Or, even worse, you learned that your answers wouldn't matter anyway. Over time, these aspects of self became increasingly associated with the experience of suffering. And when that pain became unbearable, your brilliant mind helped you avoid the pain by forgetting, burying, or denying its source.

Humans are social creatures, and part of our development is to figure out how to get our needs met within our perceived understanding of the rules. When you consider my childhood jewelry box, you can see specific things that I'd learned—hide the ring, ration the candy, don't be selfish. These unwritten rules weren't consciously chosen, but they were surprisingly effective at providing security. I learned to avoid punishment by denying things I loved, needed, and felt.

On the surface, the rules were a child's attempt to create an illusion of control. Yet deeper still, the rules held a profound wisdom that protected the vulnerability of my soul. The ring gave me a sense of empowerment and sovereignty. The candy gave me something to look forward to—a sense of hope. The money gave me a way to get love. This was how I unconsciously protected myself against hopelessness, helplessness, and powerlessness. I kept my treasures hidden—inside and out.

The entirety of my hotel room panic can be explained by the fact that I had broken one simple rule—*don't be selfish*. On the surface, I was a woman in her forties who knew she had every right to be in San Francisco. Yet in the middle of the night, I felt like a child who was going to be punished for being selfish. No matter how rational my justifications, they didn't quell my fear because I hadn't dealt with the root of the problem. I'd spent my time trying to convince myself that I wasn't being selfish, and this unwittingly gave more power to the unwritten rule. Up until that point, I'd lived with this rule hanging over my head, but I had never stopped to think about whether the rule was true or whether I should follow it in the first place.

With compassion and tenderness, I imagined myself as a small child trying not to be selfish. From that perspective, it became clear that the rule wasn't about being kind or generous; it was about serving my mother's needs and forgetting my own. Decades after my mom's death, I still became paralyzed if I wanted to do something nice for myself, always feeling unworthy and undeserving. I had lost the ability to see that my own desires deserved attention, energy, and respect. To strengthen my sense of worthiness, I needed to let go of rules that were no longer serving me. I had to accept and allow all the parts of me—even the selfish parts. This didn't mean that I stopped caring for others; it meant that I had to learn to also care for myself.

You learned to live by unwritten rules as well. Maybe you really wanted a pony, and you thought about it all the time. You'd get a pit of longing in your stomach anytime you even thought about ponies. But your family lived in an apartment building, and ponies needed grass and a place to run around, and they really didn't like to go on elevators, so you learned that it wasn't reasonable to continue wanting a pony. Maybe you gave yourself enough excuses and justifications to make yourself stop wanting one. Or maybe someone told you a story about how your great-aunt Bernice was attacked by a runaway pony. Or maybe your mom got all weepy when you asked for a pony, and you ended up feeling responsible for her sadness. However it happened, *wanting* a pony eventually became more painful than *not having* one. Whether you realized it or not, you learned that there were unwritten rules about ponies that protected you from the immediate pain of not having a pony. Eventually, this may have helped you forget that you ever even wanted a pony in the first place.

No matter who you are or how you learned, you interpreted the information around you to help you figure out who you needed to be and what you needed to do in order for you to be okay. Directly or indirectly, you learned that if you could be a little less *something* or a little more *something else*, then you'd get your needs met. Then you'd be cared for. Then you'd belong. In the beginning, it wasn't about self-worth, it was about self-preservation. You were simply implementing an exquisitely beautiful way to protect yourself, survive, and adapt to your surroundings.

One of Jung's more chilling observations was that whatever you put into the shadow doesn't sit there passively waiting to be reclaimed and redeemed; it regresses and becomes more primitive. That's why, when left unchecked, the mechanism originally meant to shelter you from harm can evolve into something that directly causes you harm.

Worthiness is the quality of deserving attention, energy, and respect.

Therefore when you withdraw attention, energy, and respect from aspects of yourself, your sense of self-worth plummets. In other words, the rules that you unknowingly put in place to protect you eventually hurt you. Your original defense mechanism may have been helpful to stop suffering in the short term. In the pony example, it may have kept you safe from despair and helplessness. However, your persistent compliance took a toll on your self-worth as you trained yourself to live within a smaller and smaller footprint of what's acceptable.

By continuing to follow the unwritten rules, you've lost the ability to access who you are, what you feel, what you need, what you desire, and what you love. As more pieces have been denied and pushed away, there is an emptiness left behind. And that emptiness hurts in a specific way. It aches with a hollow feeling of not being enough—the feeling of worthlessness. Maybe it feels like you're not smart enough, pretty enough, thin enough, or good enough. Or maybe it just feels like something is missing. Because there is something missing. Pieces of you are missing.

> **It's painful to live a life that requires you to be less of who you are.**

And eventually, often when you least expect it, what you've lost comes bubbling back up to the surface. That's why, in the middle of that road trip with your kids, you saw that pony in a field and you had no choice but to pull over. That's why you put the car in park and sleepwalked over to the white fence. That's why, for no reason whatsoever, you found yourself heartbroken and soul struck by the beauty of what was in front of you as you wiped tears from your face. And even though your kids looked at you like you'd lost your mind, that's why you wouldn't budge, and you couldn't breathe. All you could do was simply whisper, "I wanted a pony once." For almost forty years, you forgot about the damned pony, and then there it was in living color. Even though you didn't know it, your heart had always ached for that lost self. And when the love that you once felt came rushing back in, it made no sense and took you by surprise. But for some reason, leaning against that white fence, the sunlight glinting gold off the pony's back, you felt more alive than you had in a decade. That aliveness, that sense of self, of purpose, of knowing—that's what this work is about. It's about inhabiting all of yourself so that the full brilliance of life can shine through.

So instead of waiting for your lost self to organically arise on a random road trip, this work is going to help you deliberately search for what's been lost. To experience the unharnessed expression of who you really are, you need to first become aware of who you learned not to be. There are an infinite number of possible rules, but the ones that hold the most influence over your self-worth are found in a few crucial areas: identity, inner experience, security, attachment, and desire. First, we'll start by breaking down each of these categories. Then we'll look at how to break free from their limitations.

RULES ABOUT IDENTITY

You are a complex, contradictory, marvelous mess, and every single aspect of who you are deserves attention, energy, and respect. This isn't limited to the pretty pieces, the nice pieces, or the helpful pieces. It isn't limited to the successful pieces, the unique pieces, or the strong pieces.

You are a universe of ideas and details, and every single part of the cosmos of you deserves to be honored and celebrated.

Think back on who you were as a child, a teenager, or maybe a young adult, and think about the unwritten rules that you learned or that you embodied around who you were supposed to be and who you weren't supposed to be. These can be rules that you learned at home, often from your parents and siblings. Or they can be rules that you learned from your community, often from your peers, your teachers, or authority figures. These rules may have been taught directly: *be good, share with your brother, work hard.* Or you may have learned them indirectly by listening to what was criticized or praised. Maybe you overheard your parents gossiping about Aunt Betty's bankruptcy, and your unwritten rule became *don't be a loser.* Or maybe you heard your teacher praising Brent's perfect score on his math test, and your unwritten rule became *you need to be smart.*

You may discover unwritten rules around careers (*you should get a reliable job; you shouldn't be an artist*), personality traits (*you should be generous; you shouldn't be shy*), your body (*you should be thin; you shouldn't be fat*), or sexuality (*you should be modest; you shouldn't be a flirt*). There might be unwritten rules around hobbies, sports, or religion. There might be rules about who you're supposed to be within your family unit, your current vocation, or your political affiliation. You may discover rules about your gender identity, your relationship status, or your age. If you're stuck, imagine painting two self-portraits.

One portrait shows who you want people to see. Keep that portrait in your mind's eye, and try starting with *I'm supposed to be seen as [fill in the blank]*. The other portrait shows who you don't want people to see. Try starting that list with *I'm not supposed to be seen as [fill in the blank]*. There's no right or wrong way to do this; go easy and try not to edit. Whether you agree with these rules or you rail against them, the work here is to simply brainstorm and list as many rules as possible.

RULES ABOUT INNER EXPERIENCE

Your inner experience holds a world of information.

The vast expansiveness of your emotional and physical body, the innate wisdom of your heart, the tragedy of your suffering, the depth of your joy—the entirety of your inner essence deserves attention, energy, and respect.

Think back on who you were as a child, a teenager, or maybe a young adult, and think about the unwritten rules about what feelings, emotions, and sensations were allowed and which ones weren't. You may discover unwritten rules around anger, fear, shame, joy, or sadness. Maybe you learned that happiness would be punished or that sadness was self-indulgent. Maybe you learned that fear was shameful or that shame was virtuous. Maybe you were expected to endure explosive emotions and never complain. Or maybe you were told not to be so sensitive. You may discover unwritten rules that came from your experience of the emotions around you. Maybe you suffered at the hand of rage and decided never to be angry, or you felt neglected during your mother's depression and have vowed to always remain chipper. You may discover unwritten rules around pain, suffering, or discomfort. Maybe you learned that you were supposed to be tough, strong, and stoic and that you weren't supposed to be hungry, needy, or vulnerable.

The work here isn't to cast judgment. The more open and honest you are, the more you'll be able to set yourself free. Look for any rule that places judgment, marginalizes, or discounts your inner experience. If you're stuck, imagine embodying your inner teenager, and give yourself full permission to be petty, moody, and self-centered. Try starting with *I really felt [fill in the blank]*, or *I never felt [fill in the blank]*. Remember there are no right or wrong feelings here. It's all simply information to help you discover what's been lost.

RULES ABOUT SECURITY

You are beautifully and miraculously alive. Think about that for a minute.

> **To be alive means that you possess an astonishing force that needs to breathe, grow, be nurtured, and be protected. Life wants to expand, and expansion is needy.**

Security is the state of being able to satisfy your needs for self-preservation. This means your needs are not negotiable, and they deserve attention, energy, and respect. To think otherwise is to deny the life force within you. Whether you realize it or not, you have unwritten rules about your needs. These are rules about your desire for security, self-preservation, and what it takes for you to feel nurtured and protected. You may even have a blanket rule that you're not supposed to need anything at all.

Think back on who you were as a child, a teenager, or maybe a young adult, and think about the unwritten rules that you learned or that you embodied around what you were supposed to need and what you weren't supposed to need. Maybe you needed your teddy bear, your favorite doll, or a nightlight, but you learned that you weren't supposed to need comfort. Maybe you needed to be held and cuddled, but you learned that you weren't supposed to need affection. Maybe you needed to be seen, but you learned that you weren't supposed to need attention. Maybe you needed encouragement, but you learned that you weren't supposed to need praise.

Look for any rule that places judgments, marginalizes, or discounts needs. If you're stuck, imagine yourself as a sweet and innocent child, and try starting with *I really needed [fill in the blank]*, or *I never received [fill in the blank]*. The more compassion you can have for yourself, the more information you'll discover. It takes an enormous amount of vulnerability to acknowledge your deepest needs, and you may find a deep sense of grief. Be gentle with yourself and try not to censor.

RULES ABOUT ATTACHMENT

The experience of life is the experience of relationship. It is the relational experience between you and the other. Regardless of what, who, or why you love, within each relationship, there is attachment, connection, and emotional bonding.

> **Love isn't a choice. It's the connecting force between all things. It is universal and powerful. It's the thread woven between us and around us.**

Love is immortal and carries on well after loss or injury. You have an innate capacity for experiencing both sides of infinite love—through being the one who loves and through being the one who is loved. Your experience of attachment, connection, and love deserves attention, energy, and respect.

There are plenty of unwritten rules about what, how, and why you're supposed to love and rules about what, how, and why you're not supposed to love. You may even have a blanket rule that you're supposed to love everything or not love anything at all. Think of these rules as the conditions you learned that ultimately limit the way you attach, bond, connect, and love.

Think back on who you were as a child, a teenager, or maybe a young adult, and think about the unwritten rules that you learned or that you embodied around what or who you were supposed to love and what or who you weren't supposed to love. Maybe you lived in a community where traditional values were upheld, and you were supposed to love church, school, and your country. Or maybe you lived on a commune, and you learned that you were supposed to love meditation, art, and poetry. Maybe you were surrounded by financial hardship, so you learned you weren't supposed to love expensive clothes, flashy cars, or fancy houses.

Think of the rules about how you were supposed to express love. Maybe you learned not to be overly affectionate, that you shouldn't use the L word, or that love came in the form of food, money, or gifts. Think about what you had to do to get love, especially from your primary caregivers. Maybe you had to give something, be something, or deny something in exchange for love. If so, these became unwritten rules about how to earn love. Or maybe you were surrounded by affluence, so you learned that you weren't supposed to love gaudy jewelry, tacky knick-knacks, or flea markets. Maybe you lost someone you loved, so you learned that it was best not to love at all. Or maybe you never felt loved, so you conjured up rules to try to explain why.

Look for any rule that limits the capacity of your love or that limits your experience of love. If you're stuck, try starting with *I shouldn't love [fill in the blank]*, or *I would be more loved if [fill in the blank]*. The goal of this work is to gain unlimited access to the well of love within you and around you. It's to remove any restrictions on your capacity to connect and your ability to bond.

RULES ABOUT DESIRE

Your wants and desires are the mysterious forces that lead you to into life's unknown frontier. Your desires are the doorway to intimacy.

> **To speak your desires, to yourself or to others, is to give voice to your place in the world.**

Your desires are your way forward. They point to the horizon and give shape to your journey. They give you direction and lead you deeper into a life of meaning, purpose, and substance. You do not get to choose what you desire, but you do get to choose whether you honor your desires.

Through unknown forces, your desires arise from within you. This is how life unfolds and expands around you. This is how you experience the limitless possibilities of what wants to be lived through you. Your desires deserve attention, energy, and respect. Whether you realize it or not, you have unwritten rules about your wants. These are rules about what you long for, what you crave, what you hope for, and how you communicate those desires to those around you. These are rules that dictate how willing you are to acknowledge your desires and how safe you feel in sharing your desires. These are rules about being needy, rules about being independent, rules about asking for help, rules about autonomy and sovereignty, rules about vulnerability and intimacy. This category is especially important in regard to building self-worth. When you've lost your ability to connect with your truest desires, you've lost your ability to navigate, your ability to move forward, and your capacity for intimacy.

Think back on who you were as a child, a teenager, or maybe a young adult, and think about the unwritten rules that you learned or that you embodied around what you were supposed to want and what you weren't supposed to want. These are rules that limit what you intellectually, physically, emotionally, sexually, or spiritually want. Maybe you learned that your wants were superficial, unnecessary, or materialistic. Maybe you learned that sharing your desires made you susceptible to teasing or mockery, and you made a rule to not be vulnerable. Maybe you learned to be shy about expressing your wants and made a rule to stay silent. Maybe you were afraid to lose control and learned to be afraid of your wants. Or maybe you learned that you shouldn't even have desires in the first place. Maybe you learned that desires made you greedy, selfish, or self-indulgent, so you limited what you allow yourself to want.

Look for any rule that places judgments, marginalizes, or discounts desires. If you're stuck, try to access the part of you that's unfulfilled, hungry for more, desperate for change, and try starting with *I deeply long for [fill in the blank]*, or *I profoundly crave [fill in the blank]*. The goal of this work is to allow yourself unfiltered access to your inner desires, to want with abandon, and to be able to communicate these desires, even if only to your own self.

ASK AND RELEASE

Now that you have your list of rules, you get to decide how much influence these rules continue to have over your life. You can have compassion for the young self who adopted the rule and who did her best to avoid the painful consequences of breaking the rule. However, your worthy mind no longer needs to keep you small. When unquestioned, these rules hold an enormous amount of power over you. However, by bringing these rules to light, you can question their validity and render them powerless.

As you consider each rule, ask yourself one question: *Am I willing to let this go?*

Possible answers are *yes*, *no*, or *maybe*. There is no correct answer here. Each answer is valid. Try not to judge your reaction, and do your best to stay open to any feelings, sensations, or memories that come up.

"Worthiness feels all-embracing. It accepts all parts of you and celebrates every aspect of you."

To reinforce a sense of worthiness, consider keeping only what empowers you with a sense of growth, expansion, and inclusivity. Worthlessness, on the other hand, rejects, renounces, judges, and sidelines aspects of you.

Consider letting go of any rules that ask you to live within a narrower scope of yourself. Even though a rule once served an important purpose, you now have permission to let it go. This step isn't about taking action quite yet; it's about the practice of inquiry. Treat this like a meditation. Take your time with each rule. Notice if you find yourself attached to a particular rule. Notice if you feel the need to defend a particular rule. Hold the rule in your mind, and simply ask, *Am I willing to let this go?* Be curious about the nature of the rule and its influence over you. Hold the rules loosely, and imagine you have the power to question them, to have compassion for them, and then consider letting them go. To give you a better idea of how this works, let me share a few examples.

Real Stories: Annika

Annika was worried that her life had become too small. She had a few acquaintances who she'd see from time to time, but her relationships lacked intimacy. She wanted to feel worthy of love and care, yet she struggled to make meaningful connections with people. She'd been divorced for over a decade, and since then, she hadn't taken the risk to step out of her comfort zone to date someone new. She shared, "Most evenings, I fall asleep with the TV on. The idea of putting myself out there to meet someone new just sounds daunting."

When she began making her list of unwritten rules, she immediately wanted to censor herself. It felt disloyal and uncomfortable to articulate them, especially those rules that related to her mother. Throughout her grade school years, Annika would walk home from school and spend the evening hours alone watching TV while her mom was at work. "My mom did the best she could. She didn't have a choice. She had to work. We wouldn't have had a place to live or food to eat," Annika explained.

Yet thirty years later, Annika was still coming home to an empty house, and her TV was still her only companion. The irony wasn't lost on her. To be willing to take the risk to meet someone new, she'd have to overcome whatever had been holding her back.

I shared, "Sometimes we learn rules from others, and sometimes we make up our own. Think about the particular suffering of being home alone as a child. How did your brilliant mind learn to cope with that pain? What rule did it create to make being alone bearable? What were you supposed to be or feel?"

Barely audible, Annika whispered, "I wasn't supposed to complain, and I was supposed to be grateful that she had a job. I guess the rule was something like, *Don't be lonely.*"

"And if you broke that rule, what were your imagined consequences?" I asked.

"I thought maybe my mom would be mad or hurt, or maybe she would even leave." Her eyes welled with tears.

I felt so much compassion for Annika and for her mother. I could imagine how painful that situation had been for both of them. Sometimes unwritten rules are nobody's fault. They are simply ideas that were put in place in early childhood, and then over time, they gained traction as they were unconsciously reinforced.

As a girl, Annika learned to cope with her loneliness by denying it. The problem is that even though she'd denied her feelings of loneliness, she still unconsciously experienced the pain. And while that may have served her in grade school, it now continued to isolate her as an adult.

For Annika, it was important to give a voice to the unwritten rules so that she could experience a deep compassion for the child who wanted her mother and to bring the painful feeling of loneliness into the light. Until she could openly recognize how uncomfortable isolation had become, she continued to keep herself stuck in her comfort zone, watching TV.

"Let's just look at one rule: *you weren't supposed to be lonely*. Let that rule sink in, feel it in your body, and notice what happens to you when you believe that you're not supposed to be lonely."

Annika closed her eyes and inhaled deeply. She took a few rounds of breath before she opened her eyes again. She said, "I never realized how terrible it felt. I was lonely. I couldn't stop myself from feeling lonely."

"Are you willing to let that rule go?"

Annika's furrowed brows relaxed, and her tear-streaked face brightened into the slightest hint of a smile. "Yes, I guess I am," she said.

Even though it may seem simple or even insignificant, do not underestimate the power of this practice. By acknowledging one single rule and by being willing to let it go, Annika gained access to the part of her that was lonely. Her lonely self had come out of hiding. Before this exercise, Annika denied her loneliness. Night after night, she came home to an empty house, conforming to and reinforcing rules that were no longer valid. Without access to her experience of loneliness, she remained stuck in an unconscious pattern. However, once she allowed her loneliness to be felt, the door to change was opened. By regaining access to what was lost, she finally felt compelled to change her pattern and more inspired to begin taking risks.

Real Stories: Sadie

A string of failed relationships had taken a painful toll on Sadie's sense of self-worth. Her relationships seemed to follow a predictable pattern: she'd get her hopes up, thinking that she'd finally found a good guy, only to be let down a few short months later. She wanted to get married and raise a family, yet now in her midthirties, she feared that time was running out. She shared, "I don't understand why it's so impossible to meet a nice guy. I try so hard, and it always ends the same way: I end up brokenhearted, and he walks away without a scratch."

When Sadie made her list of unwritten rules, a pattern began to emerge. It sounded like she'd learned to be a nice little doormat. *I shouldn't be angry. I shouldn't be selfish. I should be nice. I should be generous.* She explained that she grew up with a demanding father, and everyone in the family walked on eggshells trying to make him happy. Her father's mood set the tone of the household. She shared, "If he was happy, we felt free to go along with our own business. But if he was upset, my

mom, my sisters, and I would drop everything and start cater-
ing to his demands. He had a volatile temper, and you didn't
want to get on his bad side."

By following rules that rendered her a doormat, she'd lost
her ability to connect with her anger, selfishness, and stin-
giness. To put it bluntly, she'd lost access to her inner bitch.
Without access to this part of her, she was likely to continue
playing out her doormat pattern with every man she met. As
a child, she'd taken on the responsibility of caretaking her
father's every need, and I imagined she was unconsciously
repeating this role in her relationships.

"What did it feel like when your dad was upset, and how
did you cope with it?" I asked.

She said, "It just felt like chaos. If my dad was upset, everyone was upset, and I'd get really anxious trying to fix it."

"What were you supposed to feel? How were you supposed
to fix it?" I asked.

"Well, I guess mostly I was just supposed to be nice. I'd try
to be positive and kind. I'd do things for my dad—bring him a
drink, make him a sandwich, ask him if there was anything I
could do. And then I'd just try to get out of his way and make
myself invisible."

"Are you still doing this with men?" I asked.

Her eyes widened, and she took in a sharp breath. "What
do you mean?" she asked.

"It sounds like you were groomed to be nice, to caretake
your father's moods, to dance around him to make his life
easier, and then to erase yourself once his needs were met.

Think back on your most recent relationship. When you got anxious or felt like he wasn't happy, did you follow a similar course of behavior?"

"I hadn't really thought about that, but maybe you're right. Whenever someone seems upset, I typically get really anxious. I try to do things for them to make them feel better. I guess I go out of my way to try to be nice."

"That's the rule you learned to follow: you're supposed to be nice. Let that rule sit with you for a second. What does it feel like? How do react when you tell yourself you're supposed to be nice? Does it feel expansive or limiting?" I asked.

She thought for a moment. "Well, I don't want to be mean."

"What's wrong with being mean if that's honestly how you feel?" I asked.

"Because people won't like me if I'm mean," she said.

"Did you know that people also won't like you if you're too nice? Especially if it's not true. People who care about you want to know who you really are. They don't just want to know the nice Sadie. They want to know the crabby Sadie and the sad Sadie and the happy Sadie. They want to know all of you. So think about that rule: you're supposed to be nice. Does it feel expansive or limiting?"

"I guess limiting. But it doesn't really feel like that."

"When you follow a rule for a long time, you might not recognize that it feels limiting. It might just feel normal to you. But imagine if you met someone who actually wanted to get to know your mean side. Imagine what it would be like if you didn't feel like doing all the nice things one day, and you told your partner that it was his turn to do all the nice things for you. Imagine what it would feel like if your partner came home upset, and you didn't feel like you had to play a role for him to feel better. Imagine if you just handed him back to himself and trusted that it wasn't your job to fix his mood."

Her shoulders visibly relaxed, and she leaned back into her chair. "I can't even imagine what that would feel like. That just seems like freedom," she said.

"So are you willing to let that rule go?" I asked.

"Yes. Yes, I am," she said.

For Sadie, she would need to let go of her need to be nice in order to get in touch with what she really wanted. Healthy relationships require both parties to show up honestly. This means that Sadie would need to be able to tune into her own needs rather than anxiously trying to caretake someone else. She'd need to be able to set boundaries for herself and for a prospective partner. Rather than unconsciously replaying the pattern she had with her volatile father, she'd need to deliberately practice a new dynamic. By being willing to stop being so damned nice, she might finally have a chance at real connection.

Real Stories: Meg

Meg wanted to learn tools for helping her team. She owned an elite gym that focused on personal training, and she was concerned that some of her trainers weren't taking the job seriously enough. She wanted them to feel inspired and self-motivated, yet she said if she wasn't there to crack the whip, she wasn't sure if any of them would lift a finger. She shared, "The whole point of our job is to motivate others to work hard. I spend so much energy just trying to motivate my team, let alone the clients, I barely have anything left at the end the day. I don't feel very inspiring. I'm just frustrated and resentful. It's overwhelming."

I wasn't surprised when Meg shared her list of unwritten rules. They all reinforced a type A pattern. *Suck it up and show up. Failure isn't an option. Work hard or go home. Sleep is for the dead. Mind over matter. Don't be a quitter. No one loves a loser.* I was exhausted just listening to her rules, let alone trying to live by them.

She shared that she grew up extremely poor and never understood why her family struggled so much to make ends meet. It wasn't until she was old enough to recognize the depth of her parents' drug addiction and alcoholism that the dysfunction began to make more sense. She said, "I just never wanted to end up like them. They could never keep a job. We lived off government handouts. It was pathetic. I promised myself I would never be lazy like that."

By trying to be the opposite of her parents, Meg's unwritten rules left little room for compassion for herself or others. While it's understandable why Meg wouldn't want to emulate her parents, she'd eliminated her ability to find positive aspects of what she called "laziness." She'd lost her ability to value relaxation, rest, and self-care while overvaluing performance, achievement, and her ability to hustle. For Meg to be an effective team leader, personal trainer, and business owner, she would need to gain access to her humanity.

"Take a moment to consider your rule: don't be lazy. Does it feel expansive or limiting?" I asked.

"Laziness feels limiting. That's why I work so hard," she quipped.

"Imagine if you were sick or injured, and you physically weren't able to work hard. What would the rule *don't be lazy* feel like then?" I asked.

"Last year, I got really sick and ended up with a kidney infection. I wasn't able to do anything. And I hated it. I kept trying to open my laptop and send a few emails, but I was out of my mind with pain. It was awful. I've never felt like such a loser."

"Okay, that's exactly what happens with this type of rule. When you're operating on an unconscious pattern of trying not to be lazy, anything other than 100 percent gets deemed 'lazy.' Even to the point where you're bedridden and sick, and you still don't feel like you're worthy of rest. Imagine if you could access the part of you that really valued self-care. The part of you that recognizes the need for nurturing, kindness, and rest. Imagine if you not only allowed that part of you, but you also saw that 'lazy' part as good and honorable and necessary. Imagine if you saw it as something to be celebrated and protected."

"I'd probably lie down, fall asleep, and never wake up," she laughed.

For Meg, she would need to let go of her overachieving

rules in order for her to connect to a deeper inner power. Once she could embrace the value in compassion and rest, she'd be able to care for herself and for her team. Rather than trying to inspire, she'd be an inspiration. By nurturing and celebrating all aspects of humanity, leadership would be effortless. Rather than unconsciously giving her parents so much power, she would finally be free to embrace a deeper sense of purpose.

YOUR WORTHY WORK: Unwritten Rules

Now it's your turn. Try to list at least two to three unwritten rules for each category: identity, inner experience, security, attachment, and desire. Once you have compiled your list of unwritten rules, you can question their validity and let them go.

As you consider each rule, ask yourself one question: *Am I willing to let this go?*

Possible answers are *yes*, *no*, or *maybe*. Remember there is no correct answer here. Each answer is valid. Treat it like a meditation. Take your time. Hold each rule loosely, and imagine you have the power to question it, to have compassion for it, and then consider letting it go.

JOURNAL PROMPTS

1. After reading through this chapter, reflect on any experiences of memories that surfaced. How might they be related to your lost self?
2. Looking back on your history, what were the formative events that led you to lose aspects of yourself?
3. What emotions surface when you think about your lost self?

CHAPTER 2

How You Lost Yourself

My daughter is home for a few days visiting from college. These precious days together are filled with her stories. Stories about her new life full of friends, classes, and work mates and her tales about the challenges and triumphs of early adulthood. We laugh together and we cry together. I am in awe of the way that she owns herself, the way that she unapologetically shares herself, the way she moves through this world. I tell her this, but she says she doesn't know another way to be. She says, "Mom, you're the one who taught me to do that." And maybe this is true. She's didn't know me when I was young. But seeing her now feels like looking into a mirror: me thirty years ago. Same hair, same face, even the same oversize flannel shirt à la 1991. She looks like me, or at least she looks like how I looked then. Except that the gift of time allows me to see a younger me through wiser and kinder eyes. She is stunningly beautiful, which is the least of it. She's also funny and smart and brave—things that will serve her far more than beauty. But what I see more than anything is that her sense of self is built on an unmovable foundation. The woman knows who she is, and she has both feet squarely rooted on the ground of this knowledge.

There are so many stories I could tell you about how I lost myself, it's hard to choose one. However, if I could sit myself and my daughter at the same age, side by side, there is one critical difference that underlies her deep-seated strength and that caused me decades of suffering. That difference? She owns her anger. She doesn't see it as wrong or dangerous. She calls on it for protection without apology. By her age, I had lost access to the part of me that was angry, and it took me a few decades to reclaim it.

Anger is critical when it comes to cultivating worthiness because anger is the signal of unfairness and boundary violation. To stand up for what I deserved to receive, I needed access to anger's wisdom. Because my anger was denied, my boundaries deteriorated, which eventually led to a complete and utter loss of self. Because of this loss, I had a very difficult time determining the nature of my relationships. Without access to anger, I had no fire in me, no protective energy. Without access to this part of me, I had no inner knowledge of whether someone wanted to use me or love me.

Before we get into my story, I want to explain something.

Every human suffers. There is no ranking of suffering. Where my childhood had physical abuse, yours may have had divorce, death, neglect, loneliness, boredom, or bullying. I do not believe there is a hierarchy in what happened to any of us. We are all hurt, and every experience matters. My stories are shared with the intention of demonstrating aspects of this work, and they happen to involve abuse because that was my personal experience. That said, regardless of our backgrounds, we all tend to lose ourselves for the same underlying reasons and in the same way. So while my stories may contrast your experience, the mechanisms at play are quite universal.

I learned to dissociate from my body early on. I imagine this was automatic in the beginning, but over time, it seemed to be something I could choose in any moment. It was a trick that served me well and helped me survive my childhood years.

My mom's viciousness had a cycle that I knew by heart. When my mom flipped into a violent rage, I would find the back door in my mind and walk through it. I could sit outside my mind until it was time to come back into myself. Sometimes I'd focus through the window to the hills on the horizon. Sometimes I'd watch the telephone cord slowly curl itself back into place. Sometimes I would focus on my bedroom light switch, the wallpaper in the kitchen, or a tree out the window. I wouldn't close my eyes; I'd simply focus on something still or serene and try to go there in my mind. I'd still have a vague impression of what was happening to my body, but I didn't have to witness the full onslaught of it.

Dissociation is a common defense mechanism for dealing with trauma, and this technique sheltered me from a reality that I couldn't tolerate as a little girl. Because of this, I was able to withstand the abuse. However, it cost me dearly in terms of being capable of integrating reality and experiencing emotions. If I wasn't there to witness the horror (and I do mean horror), then I didn't have to really face who my mother was or how she treated me.

Once the assault exhausted my mom, she would go to her room and cry. This is the point where I knew it was safe to be back inside myself. Rage coursed through my mother as superhuman strength, but the moment she flipped into tormented hysterics, she became weak, fragile, and wounded, as if she had been the sole victim of the previous crime. At the time, I didn't see her crying as an elaborate display of self-pity; I saw it as the suffering of someone who I ached to please. And more than anything, I saw her despair as a way to make myself useful and necessary in her eyes, a way to receive love.

So let me slow this down for a minute to explain how it worked. By dissociating, I disconnected from reality, which helped me keep the violence kind of fuzzy. This also helped me keep a certain fantasy of my mother alive within me. In other words, it helped me imagine her as a kind and loving mother while preventing me from having to reconcile the reality of her—a mentally ill person who tortured small children. I find this to be truly fascinating and quite a miracle that a tiny young mind automatically knows how to shelter itself from the unspeakable. My mind protected me by keeping the fear, which helped me stay quiet, frozen, and compliant in times of danger. My mind also protected me by hiding the anger. I didn't have the physical strength or stature to protect myself or to fight her. Therefore, anger could have been life threatening by igniting her rage even further, like pouring gasoline on a blazing fire.

As much as I knew what to do during the assault, I knew what do to afterward, and that was to take care of my mom. My mother would be facedown on her bed, heaving sobs sending waves through the water-filled mattress. I'd put my hand on the back of her close-cropped hair, matted with sweat and exhaustion. I'd coo and shush her and tell her, "Everything is going to be okay, Mommy." I would lean over and lay my chest against her back, my cheek against her shoulder, and I'd stretch my arms out to hug her across her shoulders and her bent arms. I'd close my eyes and breathe in her smell, and every tense part of my body would begin to relax.

It wasn't like I was overriding anger or trying to overcome the injustice. There simply was no awareness of anything other than relief that it was over. The violence was simply something that happened. In my mind, it happened to her as much as it happened to me. When I went to console her, I was not pretending to love her. Every fiber of my being loved her. True, I was afraid of her, but I also relied on her for shelter, sustenance, and life itself. She was all I knew. And this was what my experience of love had always been. I couldn't see her as someone who had wronged me; I could only see her as the one who might save me. Through these defense mechanisms, I would project kindness and love onto the image of my mother. I would see her as a small and wounded child, and I would see myself as the strong parent who needed to care for her. I didn't see that I was wounded and needed her. I only saw that she was wounded and that she needed me.

She would say, "What would I do without you, Meadow?" And oh my God, my heart would sing. I'd kiss her shoulder and lay my head against her head. I loved her more than anything in the world. And in that moment, my experience was that she loved me too. I could project onto her the love I had for her, and I could imagine her as a benevolent mother.

Dissociation, projection, idealization, denial, and repression are defense mechanisms (I'll explain more about how they work later in this chapter) that served me well in childhood. They not only kept me physically safe but also kept me psychologically safe. However, they became a huge problem in adulthood by rendering me unable to recognize when someone harmed me and by sustaining the fantasy that someone cared for me. By continuing to dissociate, by repressing my anger, and by projecting compassion where there was none, I perpetuated the dynamic of my childhood. The defense mechanisms helped me keep illusions alive rather than requiring me to face reality. When someone hurt me, lied to me, cheated on me, I'd unconsciously move toward them and try to caretake them. This happened in romantic relationships, business relationships, and friendships. When I found myself in threatening situations, I wouldn't stand my ground. Instead,

I slipped out the back door of my mind while my body froze. All the while, I felt more broken, more unloved, and hopelessly worthless.

To have meaningful relationships, to be a better parent, and to be a responsible business owner, I needed to be able to face inconvenient truths and acknowledge painful facts. I needed to reclaim and honor all my lost pieces rather than trying to protect the patchwork of untruths that kept my illusions intact. I needed to be able to clearly see reality without defending myself against it.

> ## Defense mechanisms only work when you're not conscious of them.

By bringing awareness to them, they lose their power, and you start to see the patterns that keep you stuck. For me, this meant I had to learn to stay with myself rather than slipping out the back door of my mind. It meant I had to deliberately try to access my emotions and name them as I spotted them. I'd tell myself, "I'm sad," or "I'm afraid." Naming them helped me connect them to the physical experience and break the habit of dissociation. I had to reclaim the part of me that was willing to fight so that I would be able to see myself as someone worth fighting for. I had to reclaim what I'd lost so that I could finally experience the worthiness I deserved.

DEFENSE MECHANISMS

Even though your childhood might not have much in common with mine, you probably relied on many of the same types of defense mechanisms. You may have learned to dissociate when your parents were arguing, when you were confused at school, or when you sat in the dentist's chair. You may have repressed anger because you didn't want to hurt someone's feelings, you were taught that anger was evil, or you saw your sister get in trouble for talking back. Your personal story shaped the reasons, but the mechanisms employed are universal.

In the last chapter, we discussed the fact that you lost part of yourself when keeping that part became too painful. But how does that actually happen? How does your mind go about hiding these aspects of self, and where is this information hidden?

The neurological answers to these questions are far beyond my expertise and the scope of this book, but advances in technologies such as functional magnetic resonance imaging now allow neuroscientists to confirm some of the key principles set forth by Freud,[1] namely that there are inner forces outside our awareness that influence our behavior. Simply put, your mind knows how to defend itself against pain. The processes that keep unwanted information hidden from your consciousness are known as *defense mechanisms*. Defense mechanisms are a normal, natural part of psychological development. Identifying which type you, your loved ones, or even your coworkers use can help you in future conversations and encounters.

To illustrate how this works, imagine starting out as a

completed puzzle made up of hundreds of puzzle pieces. Now imagine going through life, and every so often, some of your pieces seem to cause a lot of pain, so you take those pieces of the puzzle and tuck them into a backpack that you carry around. However, once you've removed pieces, there's now an empty space left behind, and the remaining pieces no longer fit together. You can't walk around like that because your puzzle pieces are falling all over the place. So you break out some tape and some glue, and you do your best to put yourself back together again. As you go through your life, your backpack gets heavier with all the unused pieces, and what's remaining becomes a patchwork of glue, tape, and pieces that don't quite fit together.

Defense mechanisms work similarly.

> **When part of you is lost, it is relegated to the shadow or unconscious, and defense mechanisms are the lies you tell yourself to help mask what's been lost.**

While defenses are necessary and useful in coping with the inevitable pain that goes with being human, when too deeply entrenched, they can keep you from accessing important aspects of reality that you ultimately need to face. Worst of

all, they exclude or misdirect parts of yourself that you need
for effective relationships and for strengthening your sense of
self-worth. When you repeatedly block the awareness of your
own experience, feelings, needs, and desires, you're not only
cultivating a sense of worthlessness, you are also limiting your
ability to experience intimacy and connection with others.
Worthiness is the quality of deserving attention, energy, and
respect. Therefore defense mechanisms, by definition, can
only reinforce the opposite.

There are dozens of defense mechanisms, and there are
often several supporting each other at any given time. For the
purposes of this work, we are going to focus on the defense
mechanisms that directly impact your self-worth. These are the
key defense mechanisms that keep critical information about
who you are, what you feel, what you need, what you love,
and what you really want hidden from your consciousness. To
reclaim what you've lost, it's helpful to understand how these
defense mechanisms work so that you can not only spot them
in yourself and strengthen your sense of self but also so that
you can identify which type your friends, your family, or even
your coworkers use so that you can better relate to them.

REPRESSION AND DENIAL

This type of defense works to help you erase or completely forget
painful stories, feelings, and realities by relegating them to the
unconscious. This can happen in two major ways: through
repression and denial. Repression is a motivated forgetting of

the internal reality. Denial is the refusal to admit uncomfortable aspects of reality.

Repression relates to "inside" and denial relates to "outside." In my example, I *repressed* anger, and I *denied* that I was being abused.

Denial occurs when you refuse to accept reality or facts. External events or circumstances are blocked from your conscious mind so that you don't have to deal with the emotional impact. In other words, the pain of acknowledging reality is avoided by forgetting it.

However, the problem with denial is that reality will always win out, no matter how much you try to forget about it. For example, your sister-in-law may ignore her doctor's warning about early signs of diabetes. She might refuse to change her diet, continue a sedentary lifestyle, and even increase her sugar intake. However, no matter how much she denies it, her health problem persists and will get worse if she continues avoiding reality. Or your friend might be in denial about her marriage even though she's found illicit texts on her partner's phone, he's out of excuses for coming home late, and he keeps going outside to take secret phone calls. Yet no matter how much she denies the affair, her marriage has serious problems, and her denial doesn't make them go away. Or a business owner may continue recklessly investing time and money in the business even though finances are bleak and the market is failing. Denial won't make her business successful, and it can't stop her from going bankrupt.

Repression works to evade *internal* realities. When unsavory thoughts, upsetting memories, or disturbing emotions become too painful, your psyche may unconsciously choose to hide them in hopes of forgetting about them entirely. That does not mean, however, that they disappear entirely. It only means that you're no longer conscious of the influence they have. Repressed emotions still influence behaviors, affect your health, and impact your relationships. You just may not realize the impact they are having. For example, when you repress emotions, they may surface as different emotions. Repressed anger may resurface as passive aggression, apathy, boredom, or even hatred. Repressed shame may express itself as grandiosity. Repressed fear may become confusion, anxiety, or even panic. Repressed sadness or grief can resurface as anger, guilt, shame, or even depression.

However, repression doesn't make your internal reality change; it just makes you unaware of what you're reacting to. For example, your brother-in-law isn't aware that his sarcastic comments expose his inner frustration and contempt. And the giver of a backhanded compliment doesn't recognize that their grandiosity and cruelty exposes their own insecurities. And your employee may not register that her procrastination is a passive-aggressive attempt to hide her contempt. Repression can also be quite harmful because you can no longer access critical inner information. As demonstrated in my example, when you lose access to these parts of you, you may not be able to recognize a dangerous or harmful situation.

Even though denial and repression are defense mechanisms meant to keep you from suffering, they inevitably create suffering. And this is true especially in the realm of self-worth.

Worthiness requires you to embrace all aspects of your reality. This means that any time you become aware of denial or repression, there's an invitation to reclaim part of your lost self. Worthiness is about owning your inner and outer experiences so that you can fully respond with attention, care, and respect. When you're pretending that you're healthy when you're in fact quite sick, you're not honoring the truth of who you are and what you're actually experiencing. When you're pretending that your marriage is fine when in fact your partner is cheating on you, you're not honoring the truth of what you want and what you need. When you're pretending that your job is stable when in fact your entire career may be at risk, you're not honoring what you need and what you deserve. When you're not accessing your inner experience, you've lost access to who you are, what you feel, what you want, what you need, and what you desire. Worthiness means you look at your health straight in the eyes and do what's necessary. It means you have the difficult conversation about your marriage and take heartfelt action. It means you acknowledge problems so that you can care for your future. Worthiness means you no longer ignore situations where your needs aren't being met, you no longer withstand ongoing discomfort, and you rely on your inner experience for guidance.

PROJECTION AND SPLITTING

Projection is a defense mechanism that helps your mind disown or get rid of something that feels uncomfortable and then transfers that burden to someone or something else.

Rather

Rather than seeing uncomfortable characteristics, feelings, or truths about yourself, they appear to belong to someone else. In my example, I projected love and kindness onto my mother where there may have been none. I also projected anger onto my mother while not owning my own. Think of this like a film projector, where your lost self casts stories onto a blank screen. The blank screen just happens to be a person. For example, you may have lost your ability to access anger, yet you judge your coworker for being angry. Or you may have lost access to the part of you that's willing to stand out, yet you cringe when you see someone's blatant need for attention. Or you may not see how you are critical of your partner, yet you hate when they are critical of you.

Since this defense mechanism is so common, understanding the process is one of the most powerful methods to reveal your lost self. It's also important to note that projection is both an inevitable and necessary component in psychological development, as it is one of the primary means by which we can gain an awareness of elements residing in our unconscious. This means that every time you notice yourself judging a person who upsets you, annoys you, or irritates you, it's an opportunity to consider a quality of your lost self that needs to be reclaimed.

For example, if you find that you're angry at your ex-husband and judging his ability to care for your son, it may be an invitation to consider that you are unconsciously projecting something that needs to be reclaimed in you. Maybe you find him to be selfish, reckless, or disorganized. This means you may not have access to your own selfishness, your own recklessness, or your own disorganized self, and instead of owning this part of yourself, you're projecting it onto your ex.

Okay, pause: I am pretty sure the last thing that you want to do is compassionately embrace the qualities that drive you crazy about your ex. However, when you simply look at this through the lens of a defense mechanism, you might find that it's possible this isn't even about your ex. You may find that it's about owning more of yourself. It's about reclaiming parts of yourself so that you can enjoy the full experience of what it means to be you. That means you allow yourself to own that you're selfish sometimes and know nothing is wrong with that. And being reckless is good sometimes. And being disorganized is good sometimes. Instead of finding fault in your projected image, you find neutrality in yourself.

It's also important to note that you can project both negative and positive characteristics, so it's not only important to look at who you judge to have negative characteristics, but it's equally important to look at projected positive characteristics. The next time you're scrolling through social media, watching a movie, reading a book, or listening to something that inspires you, take note of the elements that you might be projecting onto a person. The aspects that inspire, motivate, or incite envy in you may also be aspects that you're not owning in yourself. For example, a friend's Instagram post may throw you into a pit of compare and despair. Maybe you came across a picture of her completing a marathon with a big smile across her face, and it felt like a hit to the gut. That's a perfect opportunity to name the quality that possibly might be a projection. Maybe you look at the picture and think *athlete, fit, motivated,* or *winner.* The hit to the gut is an indicator that you see these qualities in her and not in yourself. This means that you've possibly lost access to the part of *you* who's an athlete, fit, motivated, or a winner. But those parts of you are still inside you, even though they have been hidden from your conscious awareness.

Splitting serves to address uncertainty and disturbing feelings by oversimplifying a complex issue and then eliminating the awareness of the disturbing feeling.

> **Splitting is black-and-white thinking—making someone all good or all bad—without leaving any room for uncertainty.**

The truth is people are complicated. They have positive traits and negative traits. This means that you can both love and hate the same person. However, it is so difficult to cope with ambiguity and confusion that you may instead move toward the illusion of certainty, even when you don't actually know, nor could you ever know.

It's easiest to understand this concept if you look at politics, sports, or even family dynamics where one side is seen as all good and one side is seen as all bad. This black-and-white thinking, or all-or-nothing thinking, is the failure to bring together the dichotomy of both positive and negative qualities into a cohesive, realistic whole.

On a personal level, this defense mechanism can make your personality as well as your relationships highly unstable. On the positive end of splitting, you have idealization—overestimating the positives while splitting off the negatives. When you idealize someone, you're only seeing the positive fantasy without seeing the reality of who they are. You can see this in my story of how I saw my mother. I kept the positive fantasy while splitting off the parts that contradicted that idealized mother.

You might also recognize this in a friend who overly idealizes new love interests. Rather than being cognizant of red flags—he doesn't return her phone calls, he's sporadically unavailable, he flirts with her friends— the problems are hidden from her awareness, and instead her idealized romance is projected onto him. This hides the reality of who she's involved with and sets her up to be blindsided when he dumps her only a few months later. After he dumps her, she no longer sees the perfect hero, and now through devaluation, she perceives the opposite extreme, where she overestimates the negatives while being unaware of the positives. By splitting off what was good, she now demonizes him by only seeing the negative.

Instead of tolerating the tension and confusion created by complexity, splitting resolves it by creating oversimplified and opposing parts, usually aligning you with one and rejecting the other. As a result, you get the comfort of believing that you know something with certainty rather than feeling confused.

> **"Worthiness requires you to honor the complicated reality of who you are and of those around you."**

Instead of splitting and projecting, you own all parts of yourself and thereby honor all parts of those around you. A worthy mind doesn't need to be right; it is willing to be wrong, and it's able to tolerate confusion. Rather than experiencing dramatic highs and terrible lows, worthiness finds beauty and peace in the subtle and ambiguous. Rather than succumbing to the simplicity of black-and-white thinking, worthiness challenges you to welcome tones of gray. Rather than distancing, judging, and rejecting aspects of yourself and others, worthiness requires you to see all aspects as complicated, interesting, and necessary parts of the whole.

RATIONALIZATION AND INTELLECTUALIZATION

Rationalization is an attempt to explain away something that you would rather not confront or accept. This defense mechanism is commonly employed to avoid feeling responsible or guilty for a choice that you've made. However, this becomes problematic when you don't learn necessary lessons due to a lack of ownership. Rationalization happens by giving reasons, explanations, or justifications that help bolster your sense of self while denying the truth about your choices.

These excuses typically remove responsibility or self-blame by externalizing reasons for why it's not your fault or responsibility. False palatable, safe, and reasonable explanations hide the true (but threatening) cause of your behavior. This allows you to feel comfortable with the choice you made or the choices others have made. It's easier to blame others or blame external reasons rather than assume personal responsibility or hold someone rightfully accountable.

In my story, you can imagine how rationalization may have helped give me acceptable excuses for my mom's behavior rather than having to face the reality of what was actually happening. For example, I may have told myself that I'd done something wrong and I deserved punishment. Or I may have told myself that my mom was having a bad day or that she was a child of abuse and couldn't help what she did. By explaining away the pain, I wouldn't have to see her as personally responsible for her choices.

Rationalization can also appear in everyday situations. For example, you may have experienced a version of this yourself when you didn't receive a job that you were hoping for. Rather than having to deal with the disturbing aspects of that reality or the feeling of disappointment and rejection, you may have explained it away by saying that you never wanted to work for that company anyway.

> **While rationalization offers explanations or little white lies that explain specific facts, intellectualization is the big ongoing lie that keeps the entire spectrum of disturbing emotion hidden.**

Rationalization is an occasional defense, while intellectualization is pervasive and can even become a point of pride. Intellectualization is the process of thinking away an emotion or a reaction that feels uncomfortable. Living in your head and being overly rational protects you from the sensations and emotions that you're experiencing in your body. This is a massive and ongoing unconscious effort to divert attention away from your inner experience and instead divert your attention to the intellect. This process removes all emotion from your responses and instead focuses on quantitative facts. Rather than fully experiencing stressful or upsetting situations, you can remain disengaged and unemotional. This may sound like a rational solution and a little like denial. However, this defense isn't denying that the circumstance happened; it's merely denying the emotional impact that the event had on you.

I know this defense mechanism well. For decades, I could easily talk about my childhood without ever feeling or truly owning the experience. I could tell stories about what happened to me, about the abuse, and I could be very specific about it, but I wouldn't feel a thing. It was similar to retelling the plot of a movie or explaining the story line of a book I'd read. I was detached and able to speak about it, yet it didn't connect to emotional or physical memories. I chalked this up to my pragmatic personality or to the fact that I was intelligent and rational.

I was unaware of how much this distanced me from my own experience. Instead of truly embodying what had happened, I could stay aloof and disconnected. However, the more I intellectualized, the more my unconscious served up nightmares, panic attacks, and even physical symptoms that pointed to my need to integrate my experience.

You may have experienced something like this when an important relationship ended by unconsciously avoiding the painful emotions involved with the breakup. Intellectualization may have helped you focus in on all the facts or intellectual reasons about why the relationship needed to end or why you are better off without that person, making a mental or even literal pros-and-cons list rather than recognizing the pain of your loss. Another example of intellectualization would be if you really wanted to launch a new business and know you need to start putting yourself out there, but instead you spend your days creating spreadsheets and task lists. By focusing on the cerebral aspects, you unconsciously avoid the discomfort of possible rejection.

Worthiness requires you to accept an appropriate

amount of responsibility and learn from your mistakes so that you can attempt to avoid the potential of similar future mistakes. It wants to know the truth about your choices so that you can change course when needed. Worthiness doesn't need to bolster itself by explaining, justifying, or blaming— it's able to own both the positive and negative sides of your personality.

> **A worthy mind isn't afraid to make mistakes. It's stable enough to withstand the discomfort of imperfection.**

Worthiness isn't a phenomenon of your thinking mind; it is an embodied experience. Rather than living in your head, which distances you from connection, vulnerability, and intimacy, worthiness wants all of you—head, heart, body, and soul.

DISSOCIATION AND NUMBING

Dissociation mentally separates you from your body or your environment to help distance you from overwhelming experiences. This mechanism helps your mind avoid the truth by escaping, numbing, or separating from reality. It can be helpful because it provides a temporary relief.

> **But in the long term, dissociation creates separation from the reality of your inner and outer experience, rendering you unable to register your feelings, needs, and desires.**

Dissociation defense mechanisms can range from mild to severe. In my story, you can see a severe example of dissociation that was helpful in childhood yet hindered my ability to navigate adulthood. You may have experienced this level of dissociation during active labor of childbirth, when you were in a car accident, or if you've been in shock after a trauma. If you've ever been addicted to alcohol or any other substance, this would also be an example of severe dissociation, because the substance facilitates separation from your body and environment.

On the lighter end of the spectrum, dissociation can look like zoning out or simply having difficulty staying present or grounded in your body. You may have experienced this while practicing yoga, attempting to meditate, or trying to focus on homework. A typical example of this is driving your car on autopilot and not really paying attention to the road ahead, even though you manage to safely make it to your destination.

Dissociation becomes a defense mechanism, however, when you are unconsciously trying to escape or avoid stressful situations or feelings. This can feel like you're detached, "out of it," or daydreaming instead of remaining present. You can also reach for something that helps you numb or cope as a way of facilitating dissociation. This can look like mindlessly picking up your phone and scrolling through Instagram, thereby avoiding how lonely you feel in your marriage. Or it can look like having a glass (or two) of wine or eating chips or cookies to help numb yourself from the stress of your workday. Or it can look like shopping (online or in real life) to help you cope with feelings of inadequacy. Any type of behavior that helps you avoid an uncomfortable feeling or situation would be an example of dissociation.

Worthiness requires you to remain present and grounded in reality. To be able to access honest answers for who you are, what you feel, what you need, what you love, and what you really want, you cannot be mentally distanced from yourself. The more you can remain present and grounded, the more you'll be able to experience the majesty and brilliance of life around you.

A worthy mind wants to recognize stressful feelings and situations so that it can appropriately respond. By being conscious rather than numb, you remain present and aware of your inner and outer experience. And sometimes that means you will experience pain. This pain is important because it helps you make decisions, react appropriately, and navigate your precious life.

BUILDING A BETTER DEFENSE

Unconscious defense mechanisms like the ones outlined in this chapter are also known as *primitive* or *immature defense mechanisms*. Research shows a strong correlation between adults who lacked nurturing as children and their reliance on primitive defense mechanisms in adulthood.[2] This research goes even further to show that the more you rely on these primitive defense mechanisms, the more they impact your midlife. Specifically, they impact your relationship with your children, marriage stability, and earned income potential.

The good news is that by consciously choosing to adopt more mature defense mechanisms, you can change course, even in midlife. Instead of being predestined for problems, you have the ability to significantly change the quality of your life. You are not meant to just sit with your suffering without relief; sometimes you will need an escape hatch. Life is full of grief, overwhelm, stress, and suffering, and you're going to need to do something that gives you temporary relief. This is where mature defense mechanisms come into play.

There are two key components to adopting mature defense mechanisms: being conscious of the defense and acknowledging the truth about reality. Immature or primitive defenses are unconscious distortions of reality. They basically obscure the truth by saying, "This isn't happening," or "What's happening isn't that bad." Mature or adaptive defenses are conscious acknowledgments of reality. They recognize the truth by saying, "This is a painful situation, and I am going to distract myself on purpose."

> **Generally, defense mechanisms are considered more mature when there's a greater ability to adapt to reality. Mature mechanisms allow you to effectively distance threatening feelings without distorting reality.**

They also build self-worth because they acknowledge your experience as it is grounded in reality rather than chasing an illusion. For example, suppression is a conscious form of repression. You make a choice to not engage with something stressful. You're aware of it, but you intentionally decide to deal with it later. For example, you might be angry with your manager, but you know it's best to wait to discuss the issue until you can speak with her privately. This reinforces worthiness by acknowledging your feelings while also pushing pause on taking immediate action.

Another mature mechanism is sublimation. This is when you transform a painful emotion into taking a healthy action. Think of this like distracting on purpose. This means you acknowledge the pain that you're in and tell yourself the truth about your need to cope. Rather than being spun out and overwhelmed, you go for a run, play piano, or start a knitting project. You acknowledge the feeling and then take an action that reinforces worthiness. You're aware of the feeling underneath, and you intentionally transform the discomfort into something productive.

There are many ways in which you can consciously help yourself cope with upsetting feelings and events. You can use humor to acknowledge an uncomfortable situation but decide to not take it so seriously. There's still an acceptance of the distress, but you choose to take it lightly and laugh about it instead. You can use altruism to make your suffering more meaningful by supporting others who also struggle with similar situations. An example of this is being a sponsor in a recovery program. However you slice it, the work here is to accept the truth and be intentional about what you do to distract yourself. By acknowledging your inner experience, you reinforce the idea that you are worth your own time, energy, and attention.

HIDE AND SEEK

Now that you have a basic understanding of how your mind hides from itself, you can take deliberate action to seek out the truth and make conscious decisions about how you want to deal with discomfort. While hiding behind primitive defense mechanisms may create a short-term illusion of comfort and may feel safe in the moment, it keeps you stuck in unconscious dysfunction and renders you unable to grow. By understanding these mechanisms, you'll be able to identify the ones that you might be using so that you can break the cycle.

Remember that defense mechanisms, both primitive and mature, are a normal response to help you cope with overwhelming feelings, memories, and ideas. So please have a lot of compassion for yourself, and tread lightly as you seek to uncover what might be hidden. It's common for people to encounter shame when they begin peeling back the layers of defense. Many of my clients are surprised, embarrassed, or quite emotional when they begin uncovering the truth. However, judging how you've defended your sense of self only keeps you stuck feeling worthless and reinforces the lost self. The goal is to be able to uncover any truth and feel neutral about it. Try to keep a sense of lightness and humor as you move through this work. When you encounter something uncomfortable, just say something like, "I was in denial? No big deal. Oh, I was projecting? Of course I was. That's normal."

The work is to acknowledge, accept, and celebrate all aspects of yourself. This means that any time you discover a defense mechanism, it's an invitation for claiming even more of who you are. By understanding how you've relied on defense mechanisms in the past, you may discover how they might be keeping you from experiencing the worthiness you deserve in the present.

As you consider each defense mechanism, ask yourself: *Where have these defense mechanisms historically shown up in my life? How did they help me avoid the truth of who I was, what I felt, what I needed, what I loved, or what I really wanted?*

Be as specific as possible.

Where are these defense mechanisms currently showing up in my life? What truth (who I am, what I feel, what I need, what I love, or what I really want) are they helping me avoid?

Be as honest as possible.

There is no correct answer here. Each answer is valid. Try not to judge your reactions, and do your best to stay open to any feelings, sensations, or memories that come up.

Worthiness feels all-embracing. It accepts all parts of you and celebrates every aspect of you. To reinforce a sense of worthiness, consider keeping the perspective of a compassionate adult speaking with a young child who is in pain. Defense mechanisms are employed to help you cope with discomfort, so be gentle as you begin to uncover what's been hidden.

This step isn't about taking action quite yet; it's about the practice of inquiry. Treat this like a meditation. Take your time with each defense mechanism. Notice if you find yourself wanting to skip one. Notice if you feel the need to defend, justify, or resist looking at the defense mechanism. That is normal. Hold the defense mechanism in your mind, and simply ask the questions. Be curious about the nature of the mechanism and its influence over you. Hold each idea loosely, and imagine you have the power to question the strategy, to have compassion for it, and then consider letting it go. To give you a better idea of how this works, let me share a few examples.

Real Stories: Macey

Macey wanted to find more meaning in midlife. As the mother of two teenage children, her life revolved around sports events, shuttling her kids to their activities, grabbing food on the go, and staying caffeinated enough to do it all over again the following day. Her professional life was just as busy. There seemed to be no boundaries between work life and home life. She took work calls on the sidelines of her boys' games, never left a text or call unanswered, and juggled helping with homework questions while answering work emails on her laptop. She felt empty and worn out, yet she didn't know what she really wanted, let alone how to go about changing her day-to-day experience. She shared, "My entire life seems to be about putting out one fire and then another until I collapse in bed and then wake up to do it all over again."

When she shared her work about defense mechanisms, she said that historically she'd relied on dissociation and rationalization. She said, "I've done this since day one in my career. I forgo sleep and push myself to the limits of what I can physically handle. And then I tell myself that this is the only way to be successful. I can't bear the guilt if I let my clients down. It's like I am always trying to prove myself, and I never quite feel secure. I know I work too hard, but I don't know any other way."

Although she was aware of the use of these defense mechanisms in her past, she was blind to how they might be creating problems in her current life. The interesting thing about worthiness is that often what you try to do to attain it is the exact thing that prevents you from experiencing it. And Macey was a perfect example of this. Rather than acknowledging her feelings of inadequacy and guilt, defense mechanisms helped her avoid them, and this cost her physical and emotional well-being. And then she'd rationalize why she needed to dissociate. It was a vicious cycle. By always being on call, she was never really present. Constantly distracted by notifications, calls, texts, and emails, she was unconsciously distanced from her physical and emotional experience. By rationalizing, she justified why she needed to keep dissociating. All the while, she kept her lost self hidden, never feeling a true sense of self-worth.

I explained this to her and asked her, "When you're numbing yourself through work, when you're on this hamster wheel of constantly distracting yourself, what truth is it helping you avoid?"

"Well, I don't have a choice. It's not like I'm trying to avoid something," she snipped.

This type of defensiveness is common and to be expected. These coping strategies are, after all, called "defense" mechanisms for a reason. They are defending someone's sense of self or defending pain. They are unconscious ways that we try to protect ourselves from the vulnerability and discomfort of reality. This is why people defend the very thing that causes them pain. My clients do this. I do this. You probably do this too. So it's best to move through this work with patience and compassion.

There's no rush to this work, and the deepest changes might not happen with a big aha moment. When you're working with the lost self, a subtle shift of awareness, a tiny spotlight to what lies hidden in the shadows, ultimately allows you to experience a more vibrant sense of well-being. As much as your psyche knows how to help itself through times of overwhelming suffering, I also believe that your psyche knows when and how to heal itself.

To soften the question for Macey, I said, "It is not wrong or bad to avoid something. It is actually quite normal and very helpful to do what you can to avoid pain. But my job isn't to help you stay small. My job is to point out where you might be stuck, where you might want to live larger, and where you might be holding yourself back. When you're distracted and busy, you don't have time to know who you are, what you feel, what you need, what you love, or what you really want. So imagine that there might be an answer that threatens your life in some way. You can keep avoiding that answer, or you can acknowledge the answer and then decide what you want to do about it. It's really about being willing to know the truth. I think you signed up for this work because you're ready to look at the truth."

Macey closed her eyes and inhaled deeply. She kept her eyes down and nodded slowly.

"Do you think distraction is helping you avoid the truth about something?" I asked.

She raised her eyes to mine, and her face softened. She

said, "I don't think I want to do my job anymore. I think I want to quit. I am so damned tired. But that is absolutely terrifying to admit."

This type of truth—wanting to quit, wanting to move, wanting to leave, wanting to walk away—is extremely threatening to maintaining the status quo of one's life. After a few decades of working with clients, I have seen time and time again that people avoid this truth because they think that once they admit it, they have to do something about it. But that's simply not the case. Acknowledging your desires does not mean you must immediately react; in fact, it's best to sit with the truth for a while so that you can get as clear as possible before you make a life-altering decision. This means you stay for as long as you can, but you stay with eyes wide open. This means you tell yourself the truth about what you want and what you don't want. It means you tell yourself the truth about your inner experience over and over again.

Macey's next steps were not about immediately resigning from her job; they were about being conscious of how her defense mechanisms were preventing her from knowing the truth. Rather than allowing herself to be constantly distracted, she set boundaries around her work, turned her phone off on the weekends, and remained present with her boys while she helped them with their homework. Rather than doing everything all at once, she intentionally tried to be mindful about separating work life and home life. Only after coming to terms with the truth would she have enough information to make the decision of whether she wanted to leave her job.

Real Stories: Lindsay

Lindsay, the mother of an eight-year-old daughter and an avid triathlete, had the outward appearance of having it all together. She started working with me to help her manage her time and be more productive. She was always on time, bright eyed and ready to learn. On the outside, she was one of those women who seem to float through motherhood with a perfect ponytail, a pretty smile, and an infinite well of patience and positivity. Yet as I got to know her through our work together, I learned that she struggled with a profound sense of shame. She shared, "I am so sick of being responsible. If I'm not running the show, no one will. My daughter struggles with her schoolwork. My husband's always gone. No matter how organized I try to be, everything seems to fall apart. I find myself snapping at my daughter over something stupid, like when she left her back-pack in the wrong place. And I'm full of resentment toward my husband because he just swoops in at the end of the evening. It feels like I have to control everything or the ship will sink. I'm so pissed that there's no one else here to help me. And then I hate myself for feeling like this."

When she shared about her defense mechanisms, she said, "Maybe repression? I have no problem feeling anger and shame. That's all I feel all day long. But I don't really know if I'm repressing other emotions or if I just don't feel them."

This is common for people who don't have a complete pic-ture of how emotions work. The human experience includes a vast kaleidoscope of emotions, not simply one or two. If your experience is limited to a few emotions, repression might be at

play. Emotions are natural sensations that play out in the theater of our bodies. They are not cerebral concepts. They offer
feedback and guidance to help us understand our lives and
give us direction to follow. They evolved to help keep us safe,
protect our loved ones, and bond with one another.

When considering repression as a possible defense mechanism, there are a few core emotions to consider: fear, anger,
sadness, and shame. These emotions are not negative or bad;
they are very important for navigating your life yet commonly
repressed. While you might not experience vivid expressions
of these emotions on a daily basis, you should be able to locate
fleeting moments of these feelings within the past few weeks.

I explained this to Lindsay and asked her, "You mentioned
anger and shame in your homework. But how about sadness
and fear? When was the last time you felt afraid? When was the
last time you felt sad?"

"I feel sad all the time. At the end of the night, I'm often
in tears, wishing I could do the entire day over again. I'm
ashamed, yes. But at night, I'm overwhelmed with sadness. I
feel like life is slipping by and I'm not able to do it right."

"And what about fear?" I asked.

"I'm not afraid. I don't have the luxury of being afraid.
Everyone relies on me because I'm such a rock." She paused to
think. "My father was an alcoholic, and my mom spent most of
the time depressed in bed. I learned early on how to suck it up
and carry on. Fear just wasn't a thing."

The interesting thing about repression is that emotions are
never really all that hidden. They might shape-shift and show

up as a different emotion. They might somatize and manifest themselves as physical symptoms. Yet however they try to hide, they are a bit like Whac-A-Mole, always popping up when you least expect them and definitely not easy to catch. Until they are seen, expressed, and understood, they can wreak havoc on both your inner and your outer lives because you are not receiving the crucial feedback they offer.

Fear wants you to pay attention. It wants to protect you from anything that threatens your well-being. It evolved to keep you alive and keep your resources intact. Fear is an appropriate response to a lack of resources—food, shelter, safety, energy, health. When fear is repressed, you're cut off from its wisdom and will miss crucial messages that point you to safety.

Fear is also about control. It's about hypervigilance and patrolling the perimeter. It's about keeping a lookout and trying to keep chaos at bay. Lindsay's entire life revolved around controlling chaos. She was perfectionistic and hyper-responsible. Even though she thought she was angry, her controlling behavior told the truth about her unconscious fear. The more afraid she was, the more she tried to keep the ship from sinking. The problem is that she had no conscious awareness of her fear, let alone what might be driving it. She'd lost access to her fear, and though she had no awareness of it, her little lost self was deeply afraid.

I explained this to Lindsay and asked, "If you allowed yourself to be afraid, what would happen? Why is fear so threatening? Think back. This is probably an old defense."

She thought for a moment and then shared, "I couldn't allow myself to be scared. My mom and dad were totally checked out. I had to help my brother and sister. They were scared...really scared. And I needed to be brave so that I could take care of them."

"But you were scared too," I said.

I could see the truth of this wash over her. Her entire body softened. "Yes, I guess I was."

"What were you scared of?"

She took a moment and closed her eyes. When she opened them, they glistened with tears. "I was afraid of being abandoned," she whispered.

For a child, the fear of abandonment is the fear of death itself. It is a terribly painful feeling to endure even for a moment. By repressing the fear, little Lindsay was able to cope with her distress so that she could help her siblings. While this was merciful and helpful in childhood, it was undermining her current relationships with her daughter and husband. Unconsciously reacting to her fear of abandonment, she became more and more hypervigilant and controlling. This created a vicious cycle. The more controlling she became, the more she pushed her loved ones away, which fueled her fear of abandonment even more.

To end the cycle, Lindsay's practice was to deliberately check for fear. Any time she found herself feeling responsible or perfectionistic, she told herself, "I am feeling fear. It's okay to be afraid." By naming it, she was gradually able to neutralize the fear rather than unconsciously reacting to it. She shared this work with her husband and her daughter so that they could be compassionate practice partners for her.

Real Stories: Janet

Janet wanted to cultivate a stronger sense of self-worth. As a single mother, she carried a lot of guilt for how much time she spent working and even more guilt for not being a better provider. She left for her morning commute before her daughter woke up in the morning and didn't arrive back home until well after her daughter had eaten dinner. Even though she worked long hours, she could never quite get ahead. She was up to her eyeballs in debt and often paid her bills late, and her self-esteem was permanently in the gutter. She shared, "It seems like the harder I try, the more I fall behind. It's just never enough. The money is spent before I even get my paycheck. It feels like all I do is work so that I can continue to work. No matter what I do, I feel like a total loser all the time."

When she shared about defense mechanisms, she said before she and her husband got divorced, she'd probably been in denial. She said, "I was completely blindsided when he left. I just didn't see it coming at all. Of course, now looking back, I see that he left me long before our divorce. I guess I just kept making excuses and believing my own lies. It was easier to think that he was working even though there was no money coming in. It wasn't until the divorce disclosures that I realized he'd lost his job months before our split, and he'd been living off our savings. I'd thought that we were financially sound, but it turned out that we were flat broke."

Although Janet was able to see denial in her previous marriage, she didn't see that it might still be playing a role in her current life. In her marriage, denial prevented her from realizing the truth about her relationship; it also kept her from seeing the truth about money. Yet denial could still be concealing the truth about her financial problems. To build self-worth and stop living paycheck to paycheck, Janet would need to be able to face reality head-on, and the best way to do this would entail getting honest about her spending.

I shared this with her, and she said, "I was afraid that you were going to say that. I have no idea what I spend. I hate opening bills, and I never look at receipts."

"Why do you hate looking at them?" I asked.

"I just know I'm not supposed to be spending. But I can't help it. I work so hard, I deserve to buy things that I want. Besides, I barely even spend money on myself. Mostly I spend on my daughter."

It is understandable and very common to want to hide from money problems. It's distressing and frightening to feel powerless and out of control. However, this type of denial and justification only leads to more financial trouble. Janet was in debt yet felt she deserved to buy whatever she wanted. She also justified her spending by telling herself that it was for her daughter. By avoiding her bills and not really looking at receipts, she kept herself from knowing exactly what she spent and exactly what she could afford to spend. This may have alleviated some stress in the short term, but it was causing detrimental consequences over the long term. To stop this pattern, she would need to study each purchase—what she spent, how much she spent—and she'd need to come clean about any lies she might be telling herself about the purchase.

I explained this to Janet and asked, "What was the last purchase that you remember making?"

"I just bought my daughter a car. She turned sixteen a few days ago, and I wanted her to have a nice car to drive."

"How did you pay for it?" I asked.

"I bought it used at a car lot and financed it." She paused for a beat. "But I can totally afford the payments."

"How do you know you can afford them?" I asked.

"Well, it's only a few hundred dollars a month." She thought for a moment. "But I guess I'm already falling behind every month, so maybe I can't truthfully afford the payments." She sighed. "I don't like that answer. That's just so depressing."

"But it's honest. And it's real. And it *is* what's happening," I said.

"But if I was really honest with myself, I wouldn't buy *anything*. And that just feels hopeless," she said.

"I know it feels that way, but if you continue doing what you're doing, it's not going to get better. Denial is keeping you stuck in a cycle of spending money that you don't have. It's kind of like pretending to be someone you're not. And that's a quick way to deteriorate your sense of self-worth. Worthiness requires you to honor who you really are—the truth about who you really are, how you really feel, and what you really need. That means that if you feel power-less, you allow yourself the grace of that truth rather than going into debt to avoid it. It means that you care for your honest needs—security, safety, comfort, love. It means that you honor exactly who you are in this moment rather than who you wish you could be."

Janet's denial was helping her avoid the feeling of hopelessness, and although this is an important emotion to acknowledge, it's exquisitely painful to endure. Her work was to find intentional and honest ways to help her cope with the feeling of hopelessness while changing her behavior to create a better financial outcome. She began by tracking her spending, listing her debts, and setting attainable goals to pay down her debt. She had an honest conversation with her daughter about what they could and could not afford. As a side hustle, she began selling items they no longer used—clothes, jackets, handbags, dishes, furniture, and knickknacks. She began listening to debt-reduction podcasts during her daily commute. When things felt too dire or when she felt the impulse to spend, she faced the truth about feeling hopeless and then intentionally put energy toward selling items online. Where she used to unconsciously spend to avoid hopelessness, she now consciously earned extra money to help pay down her debt. By redirecting her energy and allowing herself the attention and care she deserved, she immediately began reinforcing her sense of worthiness and found an authentic source of hope.

YOUR WORTHY WORK: Defense Mechanisms

Now it's your turn. As you consider each defense mechanism—repression, denial, projection, splitting, rationalization, intellectualization, dissociation, and numbing—ask yourself: *Where has this defense mechanism historically shown up in my life? At the time, how did it help me avoid the truth of who I was, what I felt, what I needed, what I loved, or what I really wanted?*

Be as specific as possible.

Then take a moment to think about your life right now. Ask yourself: *Where is this defense mechanism currently showing up in my life? What truth (who I am, what I feel, what I need, what I love, or what I really want) is it helping me avoid?*

Be as honest as possible.

Take your time. Hold each defense mechanism loosely, and be curious and open to what comes up. There is no correct answer here. Each answer is valid. Try not to judge your reaction, and do your best to stay open to any feelings, sensations, or memories that come up.

Worthiness feels all-embracing. It accepts all parts of you and celebrates every aspect of you. To reinforce a sense of worthiness, consider keeping the perspective of a compassionate adult speaking with a young child who is in pain. Defense mechanisms are employed to help you cope with discomfort, so be gentle as you begin to uncover what's been hidden.

This isn't about taking action quite yet; it's about the practice of inquiry. Treat this like a meditation. Take your time with each defense mechanism. Notice if you find yourself wanting to skip one. Notice if you feel the need to defend, justify, or resist looking at the defense mechanism. That is normal. Hold the defense mechanism in your mind, and simply ask the questions. Be curious about the nature of the mechanism and its influence over you. Hold each idea loosely, and imagine you have the power to question the strategy, to have compassion for it, and then consider letting it go.

JOURNAL PROMPTS

1. After reading through this chapter, reflect on any experiences of memories that surfaced. How might they be related to defense mechanisms?

2. Think of a time when you've witnessed someone else's defense mechanisms. Write about that experience. What happened? How did it feel? How did it affect your relationship with that person?

3. Write about your relationship to reality and the truth. What truths have been difficult to face? Where have you avoided reality in order to protect your emotions?

CHAPTER 3

What Was Lost

It was Friday afternoon and I was stuck in traffic, heading south just outside Carmel-by-the-Sea. No matter what time of day you hit this stretch, there's always a traffic delay as cars merge down to the two-lane highway that winds its way to Big Sur, but Friday afternoons are the worst. Bay Area traffic, rental cars full of tourists, trucks pulling campers, and mini-vans piled with gear all head south down that narrow stretch of Highway 1. Impatient and feeling trapped, I tapped my hands against the steering wheel to give me something to do. I turned on the radio and flipped through the stations. I just wanted to get down the coast. I wanted to be on the other side of this traffic jam. I wanted to start my weekend. That was when my husband called from home to see where I was.

"Stuck in traffic on the hill," I said.

"Oh good, you're still in town," he said, "What do you want to make for dinner this weekend?"

First, let me tell you why that was a fair question to ask. We had guests coming that weekend. We live an hour from the nearest grocery store. I was currently stuck in traffic one block away from said grocery store. I knew in the moment that this was a fair question. I also knew that a responsible adult would be able to have this conversation, go to the store, pick up food for her guests, and then drive home. I don't know why I wanted to believe that I wouldn't have to deal with feeding people or why I wanted to believe that I shouldn't have to pick up groceries.

I'd also love to tell you that this was the first time I'd been annoyed by groceries, overwhelmed by feeding people, or pissed off about what I have come to call "food management." Even that, calling it "food management," is a pretty strong clue that I may have some work to do around my relationship with food. And believe me, I have done a lot of work around this topic. But no matter how much work I'd done, this weird grocery store thing had always been an issue for me. To be more honest, food had always been an issue. And to be even more honest, weight had always been an issue. Not that I would admit this to anyone for most of my life. I didn't even admit it to myself. It was an internal battle, mostly conversations in my head that I tried to pretend I wasn't having.

I knew that I was supposed to love my body, see food as neutral, and be grateful for health. I had a daughter, for God's sake, and in front of her, I was extremely careful and compassionate about how I talked about body, food, and weight. I didn't want her to grow up with the same issues as I'd grown up with. I didn't want her to struggle like I did, always feeling like I was too big, too much, or too hungry. But off the record, I had a secret side, so secret I couldn't even admit it to myself. And that was the part of me that had continued to struggle, never feeling thin enough, never feeling that my body was good enough, and never believing that I could find peace around food.

Stuck in traffic, I felt rage burn in my chest and down my arms. I just wanted to scream. I wanted to throw my phone out the window. I didn't want to answer his question. I didn't want to have to deal with this goddamned food thing.

"I can't even think about that right now," I clipped. Short. Quick. Then I hung up on him.

Even though I was reeling with fury, I was cognizant enough to know that my reaction was out of proportion for what had just happened. I was triggered, and I knew that meant I was unconsciously reacting to the past rather than being able to consciously respond to the present. And this wasn't just a one-off; this was a trigger that I'd had for as long as I could remember. As a single mom, it hadn't come up as often because I rarely had to talk about food. But now I happened to live with an adult who expected me to be able to have conversations about groceries, meals, shopping, and dinner. I guess that is a pretty normal expectation. And my response was something like a toddler throwing a tantrum and then immediately wanting to drop to fetal position. Maybe that was not so normal.

It wasn't until I began to look at this particular trigger

through the lens of the lost self that things began to shift. I began searching for clues about what might have been lost to see if there was a correlation between those aspects and my disproportionate reaction. If this trigger pointed toward a part of my lost self, I wanted to know who she was and why she was so upset. I scanned my history for stories that matched. Was there something terrible that happened at a grocery store? No, not that I could remember. Did I get in trouble for cooking? No, not that I could remember. I spent days sorting through memories, but I couldn't find anything that mirrored this trigger or that felt the same as this powerless, raging, stuck feeling that made me want to scream.

So I took a different approach. I imagined myself as a village made up of all sorts of people. I imagined the people who were allowed to be in the village all working together to create the community of the self that I know. And then I imagined all the people who had been exiled from the village. The ones on the outskirts, the ones who were pariahs, shunned, banned. The ones who hid in the shadows. The ones who weren't allowed to come back. I imagined walking through the woods and spending time with these entities, all the aspects of self that I had lost along the way. I imagined there was a little me out there in the woods, and she was the one I needed to find. She was the one who was upset, and I wanted to know her name.

I treated this like a meditation. I knew I couldn't rush through it. This had been a sore spot for me for so long, I expected it might take a while to uncover. I'd bring this idea on my walks in the morning and observe any memories or stories that arose. I trusted that my unconscious knew how to heal itself and knew when to heal itself. And still, I wanted to know this part of me. I wanted to be able to call her by name. I wanted to love her, and I wanted to include her.

For days, the same memories surfaced on my morning walks. Me, maybe five or six years old, hiding behind a barrel in my childhood garage, stuffing a handful of raw wheat kernels in my mouth and chewing and swallowing them as fast as I could. I was hungry, and I knew my parents didn't keep track of the grain bins. I remembered the hunger and I remembered the stomachache from the raw wheat. I remembered the shame and wanting to hide.

Another image surfaced, of the weight chart hung at the foot of my bed and the scale under it. I was in sixth grade. My mother weighed me on Fridays. This determined how much food I was allowed to have over the weekend. This determined if I was good or bad. This determined if I had succeeded or failed. It didn't matter that I was a skinny little sixth grader or that my mother was obese. It was my job to be thin. And it was her job to make sure I stayed thin.

Me, in high school, at my best friend's house. Her parents had barbecued a pile of burgers with heaps of fixings. I remembered looking to see how much my friend put on her plate and then carefully studying her to see how much she ate. She ate half a burger, so I ate half a burger. I remembered being so hungry, how good those burgers tasted, and how much I wanted to eat all of them. I remembered being afraid that if I was left alone, I wouldn't be able to stop. I remembered how ashamed I was of my hunger, as if it were an unforgivable flaw. I didn't want them to know how hungry I was, desperately afraid that they'd be disappointed with me. I remembered deliberately lying, saying that I was full. I'd believed that staying hungry was the key to my belonging.

These memories were full of so much grief. It was heart-wrenching to remember how hard I tried to be thin. I was raised to believe that thin was much more than simply a body size. Thin was the measurement by which an entire life was gauged. Thin meant smart, successful, and pretty. Thin meant orga-nized and inspiring. Thin meant a big house and a nice car. Thin meant beautiful clothes and fancy jewelry. Thin meant you'd be chosen and loved. Thin meant you'd have friends and money. Thin meant you'd be popular and probably even famous. Thin meant you'd go to heaven (I'm not kidding), because God loved thin people. Thin meant everything good. And everything good came at a price: I simply had to stay hungry.

I thought about these stories and the common threads between them. I spent hours walking with these stories, imag-ining the part of me that had been exiled from the village. Who was the girl who secretly ate handfuls of wheat, hidden in the garage? Who was the girl who stood on that scale hoping that the number would be lower than the previous week? Who was the girl who sat at the table with the pile of hamburgers?

She was the Hungry One. The moment I heard her name, the Hungry One, tears filled my eyes. Of course she was the Hungry One, and of course she couldn't be in the village; she'd been exiled long ago. I'd spent a lifetime denying that I was hungry, forgetting that I was hungry, dissociating from a body that was hungry. I didn't remember when I'd lost her, but I knew I needed to find her. I knew I needed to reclaim her. I knew I needed to celebrate her.

I understood why I'd lost the Hungry One. To be conscious of constant hunger had been mentally intolerable. To be aware of the hunger pangs had been physically unbearable. I couldn't keep the Hungry One if I hoped to become the Thin One. I'd believed the Thin One held the keys to my self-worth in addition to all the things I'd ever wanted. So in exchange, I'd exiled the Hungry One, and my psyche fiercely protected me from recognizing this loss.

The simple question "What do you want to make for dinner this weekend?" unconsciously put me face-to-face with the Hungry One. On the surface, I felt triggered and pissed off. But underneath all that, the question required me to either admit that the Hungry One existed or deny her once again. This is why I hated to discuss groceries, meals, and food planning. This is why I'd made food into a thing that required "management." This is why I still wanted to distance myself from food, from cooking, from nourishment, and from acknowledging my needs. I'd lost the Hungry One, and the only way forward would be to welcome her back to my village of self.

THE VILLAGE OF YOU

Imagine yourself as a village, a community of members who make up your personality, your behaviors, your wants, your needs. Think about the countless aspects of the village of you. Inside the walls of the village are those who were deemed acceptable. The ones who didn't threaten harm or put you at risk. These were the safe ones, the ones who followed the unwritten rules. The ones who shape-shifted themselves to please others. The ones who were wanted and allowed. The ones who felt the appropriate feelings. The ones who needed only what was permitted. The ones who loved according to the agreed-upon rules and the ones who only wanted things that were acceptable to want. Some of these villagers were ones who your defense mechanisms created. Some of them were ones who the mechanisms defended. Inside the walls were the ones who were sanctioned by the council of consciousness. They were the ones mandated to be in the village. They were the ones who you tried or hoped to become. They were the ones who held perceived value, worth, and merit. Or maybe they were simply the ones who were left after you discarded the rest.

Now think about the ones who were exiled from the village and sequestered to the shadows. These are the villagers who make up the lost self. These are the ones who at some point had put you at risk or caused too much pain for you to endure. These were the ones who were cast out and banished. These were the dangerous ones, the ones who broke the unwritten rules. The ones who didn't feel the appropriate feelings. The ones who needed more than what was permitted. The ones who loved the wrong things and followed the wrong rules. The ones who wanted things that were unacceptable to want. Some of these villagers were ostracized through unconscious defense mechanisms and some through intentional selection. Eventually, the outsiders were the ones who were relegated to the unconscious. They were the ones who you hoped and tried to never become. They were the ones who held perceived flaws, worthlessness, and inadequacies.

Now imagine that for every villager who was outcast, there was a corresponding villager who remained within the walls. And for every villager who lived within the walls, there had to be a corresponding villager outside the walls. For every unwritten rule, there were two compensating villagers created: one inside the walls who you were supposed to become and one you weren't supposed to become who was cast to the shadows. In other words, there couldn't be a bad villager outside the walls without a good villager remaining inside the walls, or vice versa. There couldn't be a right villager inside the walls, without a wrong villager being evicted. For every unwritten rule that you learned to follow, there was a villager who remained and one who was rejected.

This doesn't mean you became all the traits within the walls and you avoided all the traits outside the walls. It actually turns out to be the opposite.

The more you try to avoid the outcast qualities, the more they persist.

For example, the harder you try to avoid being the Controlling One, inevitably the more controlling you become. And the more you try to become the idealized qualities, the more elusive they become. For example, the more you try to become the Nice One, the harder it becomes to reach the ever-moving goal of being nice.

When I did this work, I realized that the more I ignored the Hungry One, the more afraid of hunger I became. I wasn't aware of the thinking behind this, nor was I aware that my perception of hunger was lost to me. But physically and psychologically, the fear was very real. I had a deep fear of being hungry, and I had many bad memories of being hungry as a child. So I consciously knew that I was afraid of being hungry. But I chalked it up to PTSD. I just couldn't handle the feeling of it, and I figured it was some sort of leftover trauma from childhood. Without real-izing it, I did whatever I could to avoid hunger. I wouldn't even let myself move in the direction of possibly becoming hungry. However, I had no conscious awareness that I was disowning and pushing away this aspect of self. Owning my hunger was a blind spot that I constantly navigated around and never quite recognized. Interestingly, the more I tried to avoid being hungry, the more often I felt compelled to eat. In essence, the more I tried to avoid the Hungry One, the more powerful she became.

On the flip side, the more I tried to become the Thin One, the more discouraged I felt. I felt like something was intrinsi-cally wrong with me. I could never quite get to the thing that I thought I was supposed to be. If the goal was to lose the Hungry One in order to gain the Thin One, it didn't work. The more

I tried to avoid being hungry, the more often I wanted to eat. And the more often I ate, the more difficult it became to be the Thin One. I couldn't admit to myself that I was chasing a carrot I'd never be able to bite.

I couldn't even admit to myself that the old unwritten rule of "you're supposed to be thin" was something that I secretly still believed. I'd tried to pretend that I didn't believe this anymore, that it didn't matter, and that every body was beautiful. Except way down deep inside, I'd always heard a voice that said, "Yes, every body except for yours." So even though I tried to convince myself that the Thin One held no power, I couldn't release myself from the grip of disappointment of never quite becoming her. The more I tried to become her, the further away from her I found myself. The more I tried to pretend I didn't care, the more disappointed in myself I became. In essence, the more I wanted to be the Thin One, the worse I felt about myself.

Worthiness wants to embrace, welcome, allow, and own all aspects of self.

> **There's no such thing as being more worthy or less worthy.**

Worthiness is the quality of deserving time, attention, and respect. And that applies to all villagers inside and outside the borders. Worthiness requires no borders and no walls. It welcomes and embraces all villagers. It wants everyone to be included.

The work here is to remove the unconscious judgments of good and bad, right and wrong, so that every villager is not only neutral but also regarded as necessary.

> **Worthiness doesn't happen by exiling the bad parts and then exalting the good parts. Worthiness happens through embracing your whole self.**

It wasn't until I saw the Hungry One and the Thin One as polarities of the same idea that something finally clicked. The underlying idea of both polarities was that my body needed to be controlled. Control the hunger and control the weight. I couldn't deny the Hungry One and try to become the Thin One—that had never worked. I couldn't deny the Thin One while allowing the Hungry One because they were part of the same system. Holding one aspect as a virtue and the other as a sin will never set you free, because seeing one as light automatically casts the other one as dark.

To come to peace with these aspects of me, I would need to welcome both the Hungry One and the Thin One. Instead of seeing hungry as bad and thin as good, I'd need to see they both held good and bad within them. The Hungry One was good because she helped nourish me. She was needed because she kept me alive. She was driven and wanted to thrive. She was not worth banishing; she was important and necessary. The Thin One wasn't as holy and almighty as I'd been taught to believe. She had plenty of flaws. She wasn't smarter, more successful, or more perfect than the Hungry One. She wasn't the key to all life's joys. She was actually the key to a lot of my shame and disdain for my body.

However, the work isn't to simply flip-flop. Worthiness is strengthened by embracing both the light and the dark. I didn't need to banish the Thin One and welcome the Hungry One. I had to welcome every aspect on the spectrum of that polarity. I had to allow the one who wanted to control the body, and I had to allow the one who just wanted to say fuck it. I had to allow all the hunger to be present and felt, which also required me to allow myself to be present with the feeling of being nourished. Instead of trying to avoid being hungry, I allowed myself to experience hunger with curiosity and interest in how my body communicated its needs. I allowed myself to eat meals out of kindness, honoring the needs of my body and deliberately responding to those needs. I had to see that the Hungry One wasn't all bad and wasn't all good. She was just a part of me that had information. She was important and needed to be included.

Respectively, I also had to take a good look at the Thin One. There were great things about her and terrible things about her. But more than anything, I needed to respect that she was part of the village of me. I needed to understand that she had a voice and power and that pretending she wasn't there would never help me feel whole.

In the end, this work wasn't about food, and it wasn't about weight. It was about being generous with myself, being kind to my body, and doing the work to welcome all parts of me. By dropping the shame and extending each villager an invitation to belong, I began to feel an expansive sense of trust, compassion, and affection for my physical body. I wanted to honor it, protect it, feed it, and respect it in a different way than I had ever experienced.

However, it wasn't until I was confronted by the same trigger that I realized how profound the shift had been. A month after doing this work, I'd had a hectic week getting ready for a getaway with a few of our friends. My husband and I were joining three other couples for a weekend at a cabin in the woods. As we got closer to the weekend, our once quiet texting thread became a flurry of messages. We talked about what to pack and about travel plans and began organizing when people would be arriving at the cabin. Dozens of texts flew back and forth before the one that stopped me in my tracks.

"Okay, guys, so what are we doing for food?" Jodi asked.

I looked at the blue bubble on my iPhone and held my breath, waiting for the familiar wave of panic and rage. I took another breath and then another. I watched text after text come in.

"We can make a pot roast," Sara said.

"I'll make a cobbler," Amy chimed in.

"Can one of you guys bring up salad stuff?"

I stopped reading and closed my eyes. My breathing was calm. My chest wasn't hot. I felt relaxed, fine. Weirdly normal. *Okay, guys, so what are we doing for food?* I silently repeated this question to myself. I thought of my little six-year-old self, hiding behind the grain bins with handfuls of wheat kernels. I imagined what it would be like if I could just hold her close and cook her a nourishing dinner. I thought of my sixth-grade self and imagined ripping that stupid weight chart from her bedroom wall and invited her to the table as well. I thought of my teenage self and promised her that no one was going to love her any less for being hungry. This was how I determined what I needed to bring to the cabin, food for all the Hungry Ones from my past. These were the ones I checked in with, the ones I wanted to honor. These were the ones who needed to be fed. And where I once felt unreasonably furious and triggered by being asked about meals, I now felt open and receptive to the question. Where I once was blind to my own needs, I now felt privileged to have finally met this lost part of me and to be able to care for this tender part of me that desperately needed care.

I envisioned the dinner table with all my past selves and imagined asking them questions. *What do you want for dinner? How would you like to be fed? What are you hungry for?* I stayed quiet and listened for answers to arise from within me. As they surfaced, I heard, *I just want to have enough. I want lots of food. I want to make sure there's enough for me. I don't want to worry.* The answers sounded like those of a little girl who didn't trust that she'd be fed, who was scared she wouldn't be cared for. These answers were raw and vulnerable. Once I heard them, I felt nothing but compassion for what I'd lost. I wanted to protect this self, myself.

When I welcomed all the memories of the Hungry One to join me, the task of meal planning felt different, more intentional. I was worthy of being fed. Food no longer felt like something to manage; instead it felt oddly sacred. It wasn't just a grocery list for a shared dinner at a weekend getaway. It was an offering of love, respect, and devotion to myself, my past, and the beautiful people who would be gathering at the cabin.

"We'll bring burger stuff," I added to the texting thread, remembering that huge pile of burgers from thirtysomething years ago. I made a pact with all the hungry selves that there would be plenty and that I would be nourished and cared for. I even went so far as to precook individual meals for myself for the entire weekend, just to prove to all the lost hungry ones that there would surely be enough. I chopped carrots and cooked chicken, I made rice, and I packaged everything into labeled meals for myself. From the outside, this might sound a little over the top or even a bit humorous. But here's the thing about those lost aspects of self: when you find one and you name her and understand her and you know what she feels, wants, and needs, you feel a deep and meaningful reverence in caring for her. You recognize her worth, and you would do anything to honor it.

NAMING YOUR VILLAGERS: UNWRITTEN RULES

Think of your whole self as a village made up of all different characters. Think of the villagers who remained in the village as well as the ones who were exiled to the shadows.

> **Imagine that each part of you—a characteristic, a role, an idea, a feeling, a need, a desire—is an important entity that deserves to be named.**

Before you can reclaim, own, or celebrate these aspects, it's important to first honor and even to grieve what has been lost. By naming the entity, you begin the process of understanding her, recognizing her, forgiving her, and maybe even loving her. Each entity holds invaluable information, important stories from your history, and insights to consider for your future.

First, review your unwritten rules from your worthy work in chapter 1. Look over your rules about identity—who you were supposed to be and who you weren't supposed to be. For each rule, name the entity who remained inside the village walls and the compensatory entity who was exiled from the village. For example, if an unwritten rule said you were supposed to be compliant, you might name the entity within the village the

Doormat. And then perhaps you'd name the exiled entity the Boss, the Bitch, or the Rebel. The names will be unique to you and your experience. It's not important that you find a grammatically correct antonym. It's more important for you to imagine both entities as clearly as possible.

Name the entities who correspond to your list of unwritten rules, rules about inner experience (what you were and weren't supposed to feel), rules about security (what you were and weren't supposed to need), rules about attachment (what you were and weren't supposed to love), and rules about desire (what you were and weren't supposed to want). As you work through the rules, it's common to have repeated names. You may find that you have the Stoic One and its opposite the Sensitive One in several categories. Or you may find that you have the Success and the Failure in several categories. This is fine; just list them once. This step is simply about naming as many individual entities as you can find. Take your time as you move through your notes. This isn't about aggregating a list of words; it is more about naming aspects that need to be seen and recognized. Use names that work for you, names that are meaningful to you, names that help you recognize this exact part of the village of you.

NAMING YOUR VILLAGERS: DEFENSE MECHANISMS

Next, look over your homework from chapter 2 about the defense mechanisms. For each example from your homework, name the entity who remained in the village and the compensating character who was exiled from the village. Remember, defense mechanisms are lies that help mask a truth that's been lost. So for defense mechanisms, you'd name an entity who represents the lie and an entity who represents the truth.

For repression and denial, you'll name an entity for what was hidden and the entity who took its place. For example, if denial helped you believe your marriage was fine when it wasn't, you'd have two entities to name. One would represent the lie, "My marriage is fine." Maybe you'd call this entity the Pretender, or the Faker, or the Hopeful One. The compensating entity would represent the truth, "My marriage is in trouble." Maybe you'd call this entity the Cheater, the Heartbroken One, or the Fighter. Ultimately, the names will depend on your history and your personal experience. In an example of repression, the first entity represents the truth of what was repressed. If you repressed anger, one entity would be the Angry One, and the compensating lie might be called the Aloof One.

For projection and splitting, you'll name the entity who was split off or projected. For an example of projection, if you cringe when someone obviously seeks out attention, you might call that entity the Exhibitionist. The compensating entity might be the Invisible One. For splitting or black-and-white thinking, you'd name both sides of the split, the black and the white. For example, if you see your ex as all bad, you might call that entity the Devil and the corresponding entity the Angel. Again, the names should be meaningful to your personal experience.

For rationalization and intellectualization, you'll name

the entity who corresponds to the lie and the entity who corresponds to the facts. For example, if you rationalized not getting the job by telling yourself that you didn't want to work there anyway, one entity would correspond to the lie, maybe the Indifferent One, and one entity would correspond to the truth, maybe the Rejected One. For intellectualization, you'll name the overly rational thinking entity, maybe the Computer, and the corresponding entity would be the one who feels the emotions, maybe the Emotional One.

For dissociation and numbing, you'll name the entity who corresponds to the painful truth and the corresponding entity who wants to escape. For example, if you notice that you often dissociate while you're at work, you'll need to find what painful truth you're avoiding there. Maybe you're avoiding feeling incompetent, and you're worried that you'll lose a critical client, so you might name that entity the Incapable One, and the one wanting to escape that feeling might be called the Exhausted One. For a numbing example, if you check out by using alcohol, food, TV, gaming, or social media in the evening because you can't stand the drudgery of your home life, the painful truth entity might be the Bored Housewife, and the one who wants to escape might be the Wild Woman.

Again, this work is simply about naming as many individual entities as you can find. Take your time as you move through your notes. It's better to have a shorter list of names that have a strong emotional resonance rather than a long list of words that have no personal meaning to you.

WELCOMING THEM HOME

Now that you have named the entities who were lost and those who remained, the next step is to remove any metaphorical walls or emotional borders so that every aspect is acknowledged as a necessary and meaningful part of you. The work is to welcome and include every aspect that you've denied, pushed away, repressed, controlled, or silenced.

> **Through the process of naming and welcoming each named entity, you'll begin to see the lost self as a group of individual characteristics that want to be heard, understood, and respected.**

Worthiness is about broadening your understanding of who you are, welcoming and including all parts of you.

The goal of this step isn't necessarily to see each entity as all good or completely positive. It's more about seeing that each entity has both negative and positive qualities. It's about recognizing each entity has both harmful and helpful qualities. It's about holding the complexity, ambiguity, and value of each entity without having to evaluate it. This process is about opening your mind and heart so that you can be flexible with aspects of the lost self. It's about removing shame, regret, and disappointment so that you can embrace the gifts of each aspect. It's about removing stigma, judgment, and criticism so that you can broaden your sense of self. The more aspects you can own, appreciate, and welcome, the more expansive your experience will be.

Please take your time with this. This work is intentional and thoughtful. Look over your list of entities and choose at least three entity pairs. Each pair will include one name that was exiled and the corresponding name that remained. You're looking for any that feel like they have a particular charge—positive or negative. These might be entities who you may feel reluctant or even resistant to owning. Or they might be entities who you've put a lot of effort into trying to become or to avoid.

Take a moment and imagine having a conversation with a specific named entity. For each entity named, you will say their name. As you say their name, imagine this entity as a person, a friend, a part of you who was exiled to protect you from suffering, or a part of you who remained behind to try to help you. No matter which side of the wall this entity fell on, when you say their name, have compassion, respect, and reverence for them. And then when you're ready, you will welcome them into the village of you. Close your eyes, picture her in your mind, and take the time to really listen for the answers that arise from within you.

Ask her:

- *Who are you?*
- *What do you feel?*
- *What do you need?*
- *What do you love?*
- *What do you really want?*

It's also important to note that some names will be easier than others. You might find that you don't want to have a conversation with the Stupid One, the Frumpy One, or the Insignificant One. You might find an inner resistance to welcoming some of the characteristics. That is normal and to be expected. In the next chapter, you'll take this work even further. But for now, the work is simply to name them and to have compassion and understanding for them so that you feel open to each characteristic within you. To give you a better idea of how this works, let me share a few examples.

Real Stories: Margot

Margot had recently quit drinking. She was ready to enrich her newly sober life and eager to invest in personal development. As a mother of two little girls, she wanted to improve her physical health and her emotional health. She regretted the years that she'd spent numbing out in the evenings and desperately wanted to be a better mother. She felt unsure about herself, guilty about the choices she'd made, and like she was letting her children down. She shared, "I stopped drinking because I wanted to be there for my kids. But I still struggle. I don't really know who I'm supposed to be for them. I just don't trust myself to make good decisions."

When she shared her list of villagers, she said that she had purposely given up the Rowdy One when she stopped drinking. While this choice felt noble in the beginning, after a while, she felt like she'd lost an important piece of who she was. She said, "That's what drinking had given me, a reason to be wild, a reason to feel free. It was like my little secret rebellion where no one had power over me. But I took it too far, and now that I've stopped drinking, I think I've completely lost that side of me, and that makes me really sad."

It might seem helpful to demonize a characteristic, especially if you're trying to quit a harmful habit. However, by trying to rid yourself of that quality, you inevitably give it more power. Instead of keeping the Rowdy One and finding new and sober ways to feel wild and free, Margot tried to completely erase this part of her. Her sadness was a clue pointing to the significance of this loss. Her waning self-worth was also a clue pointing to what might need to be reclaimed. There was still a part of her that longed to feel wild, rebellious, and free, and it was important, even crucial, to her well-being.

To be clear, this had nothing to do with being intoxicated. You can be wild, rebellious, and free and be stone-cold sober. In fact, I would argue that the only way that you truly feel wild, rebellious, and free is in a sober state. Otherwise, you'd be dissociated through a substance, which is a dulled-down and artificial attempt to experience an illusion of freedom rather than the real experience of it.

If the Rowdy One was the name of the part of her that wanted to escape, Margot would also need to name the entity who corresponded with the painful truth of the situation. Her defense mechanism had been numbing in the evenings while at home with her kids. This meant there was a painful truth in that area of her life that she would need to name.

I explained this to her and asked, "If you aren't supposed to be the Rowdy One, what are you supposed to be? What's the name of the compensating entity?"

She answered, "I think the closest word to it is *tamed* or maybe even *domesticated*."

"Which one has more emotional charge for you? The Tamed One or the Domesticated One?"

She laughed and made a gagging face. "Oh God, the Domesticated One makes me want to barf."

This is how you know you're onto something important. Sometimes you'll be resistant, angry, or even sad about specific characteristics. Sometimes you'll be downright repulsed. And that's the work of the lost self: the further into the shadow, the more you'll want to adamantly deny, avoid, or even rail against welcoming and neutralizing these aspects.

Margot was willing to reclaim the Rowdy One but completely disgusted by owning the Domesticated One. However, they were characteristics that related to each other, to her history, and to her feelings of worthlessness. Her work wouldn't be to only honor and respect the Rowdy One. Otherwise, she would be casting the Domesticated One to the shadow.

I explained this to her and suggested that we start with the Domesticated One. She crinkled her nose in protest but conceded to doing the work.

I said, "Picture the Domesticated One in your head. Think about what she looks like, what she's wearing, where she comes from, and what she believes. Do your best to see her as neutral. She's not good and she's not bad. She's simply a part of you, and your work here is to get to know her. When you've got a good picture of her in your mind, let me know."

She thought for a moment and then nodded her head.

"Describe her to me," I said.

"She's the perfect picture of a 1950s housewife. Her hair is pulled back in a flawless ponytail. She's wearing heels, a dress with a cinched-in waist, and a checkered apron over her dress. She's who my mother told me I should be. She's the picture of the perfect mom. The perfect housewife. The woman who takes care of everything and looks good doing it." She rolled her eyes in mockery.

"Okay," I said. "Try not to judge her, and simply be open to who she is. Every part of you is important. Every part has something to offer you. Now, step into her shoes, become her in your mind, and answer these questions. Who are you?"

She took a moment before she answered. "I am a woman who takes care of the kids and the house."

"What do you feel?" I asked.

"I feel proud of myself," she said.

"What do you need?"

"I need structure," she said.

"What do you love?" I asked.

"I love my kids, my life, my home," she said.

"What do you really want?" I asked.

"I really want a plan or a system to follow," she said.

I waited for a moment so that Margot could absorb these answers and take them in. Even though Margot didn't originally want to reclaim this aspect, she had a newfound respect for this aspect once she answered the questions from the perspective of the Domesticated One. This didn't mean she had to start acting like a 1950s housewife; it simply meant there was a part of her that felt pride in taking care of the house and kids. There was a part of her who wanted structure and wanted a plan. By naming and honoring this part of her, Margot could be more open to bringing forward these aspects in herself.

On the flip side, when Margot answered the questions from the place of the Rowdy One, she found that she had a corresponding part of her that thrived without rules and structure. This was the part of her that felt free, needed flexibility and play, loved to create, and deeply desired being in nature.

Originally Margot had deemed the Domesticated One a product of a bygone era and the Rowdy One a product of her drinking. However, both entities held important information for her to consider. Rather than deeming one side bad and one side good, Margot learned that she needed to reclaim and celebrate both. She needed order, and she needed freedom. She loved her domestic life, and she loved her wild self. Rather than trying to avoid herself, she relaxed into herself. Instead of trying to eliminate these qualities, she learned to recognize them, lean into them, and welcome them.

Real Stories: Maria

Maria wanted to learn how to set better boundaries. She felt like she could never get far enough away from her overbearing mother. Even though she'd moved across the state, her mother's manipulations still affected her on a daily basis. No matter how often she spoke to her mother or how often she visited, her mother was never satisfied. Maria felt guilty and selfish and didn't know how to end the cycle. She desperately wanted to feel free to live her own life, yet she constantly felt pulled into her mother's dramas. She shared, "I moved away so that I could breathe, but my mother just ups the ante. She's perpetually wounded and makes me feel guilty if I don't swoop in and save her. I know it's dysfunctional, but I don't know how to stop this dynamic. She's frail and old, and there's no one else who will help her. It's all on me."

Maria shared that the entity with the strongest charge was related to an unwritten rule from her childhood where she was supposed to be a pillar of strength for her mother. Similarly, she was supposed to have no needs while her mother had all the needs. Not only was she supposed to care for her mother, she was supposed to help her, fix her, save her. According to the unwritten rules, Maria was supposed to be the Hero and her mother was always the Victim. This was the dynamic that had played out all through Maria's childhood and now well into adulthood. The more Maria tried to become the Hero, the more exhausted, overworked, and overburdened she became. She said, "The thing is, this dynamic isn't only happening with my mother. It's also happening with my coworkers and in my friend group, and it's even happening in my dating life. Now that I think about it, it seems like I'm surrounded by people who always need me to help them."

This is what happens when we idolize an aspect and lose another. Maria was well aware of how she had embodied the role of the Hero—she prided herself on how she helped others, how she gave selflessly to her friends, and how she was someone people could depend on. However, she didn't see how this role had kept her stuck in a web of dysfunction with her mother and how she ended up recreating that dysfunction at work, in her friend group, and in her dating life. In her relationship with her mother, Maria saw herself as the Hero—the one admired for rescuing those in need—and her mother as the Victim—the one who had been hurt and preyed on and who needed to be rescued.

However, no one is ever completely a hero, nor are they solely a victim. We all have moments of bravery and greatness, and we all have moments when we need the help and care of others. Maria had propped up the idea of always being the rescuer and had completely lost the part of her who also needed to be rescued. However, worthiness isn't solely about being heroic, great, brave, or strong. Worthiness also requires the ability to honor wounds, to seek help, to own your vulnerabilities. To free herself, Maria would need to reclaim the parts of her that had been hurt, manipulated, and exploited. In short, Maria would need to honor the part of her that was the Victim.

I explained this to her and suggested that we start with the Victim as an entity who she had perhaps lost and, as a defense mechanism, she might be projecting onto others. She looked stunned. She had never even considered the idea that she too might need rescuing. Nor had she imagined that she might be projecting this concept onto others.

"Do you think there's possibly a part of you who is also a victim?" I asked.

Maria lowered her gaze and took a moment to think before she said, "I don't think I've ever had that luxury."

"Interesting word choice," I said. "How is being a victim a luxury?"

"I don't mean it to sound disrespectful. I meant that I never had the option of being the one who had been wronged or the one who needed to be cared for," she said.

"If you've lost access to the part of you who has been wronged, you've also lost the ability to protect this part of you, to help this part of you, and to receive help for this part of you," I said. "In other words, I think you have a Hero within you. We all do. However, you've lost access to the Victim within you. You see it in everyone else, but you deny it in yourself. I think there's a part of you who has been hurt, who feels manipulated, who is tired of being used. I think this part of you wants to be reclaimed. I think she wants you to rescue her. To rescue yourself."

A wave of recognition passed across Maria's face. "Oh," she said. "Is this why everyone looks to me to fix their problems? I'm the one who fixes and never needs fixing? I'm the one who gives and never receives?"

I waited in silence for Maria to find her own answers to the questions she posed.

After a moment, she gave me a half smile and nodded her head. "Okay, so how do I change this?" she asked.

Reclaiming an entity called the Victim might not sound very sexy or uplifting, but it's profoundly helpful when you're stuck in a dynamic of enmeshment and codependency. This work is about allowing all aspects to have a voice and engaging with every part of yourself. Instead of projecting onto others, you own it within yourself. Instead of striving to be a better, stronger, improved version of yourself, you allow yourself to be as is. This happens through the work of reclaiming the good and the bad, the beautiful and the ugly, the impressive and the embarrassing. By neutralizing all aspects of yourself, you not only change how you feel about yourself, but you also change how you feel about others.

Maria shared her work after spending time with the idea of reclaiming this aspect of herself. When she asked, *Who are you? What do you feel? What do you need? What do you love? What do you really want?*, she found that the Victim was the wounded part of her, the one who felt betrayed, the one who needed to be cared for. This part of her loved her mother but really wanted her mother to be the parent. This part of her wanted the luxury of being a child. She shared, "When I found these answers, I just started to weep. I felt this deep well of grief and a profound sense of love for this part of me. At first, I didn't believe that anything would come from this, but I think something shifted inside me through this process. I can't deny this wounded part of me anymore. When my mother called this morning, I just let it go to voicemail. I wasn't angry. I wasn't hurt. I just didn't have the strength to take on her problems today. I realized that I needed to take care of myself first."

When she shared her work around the corresponding entity, the Hero, she was surprised to find just as much emotion and tenderness. She shared, "I'd always thought that the Hero could handle anything, but when I stepped in her shoes and answered the questions, I was shocked at what I found. She is the part of me who is scared, the part who feels abandoned. She needs to be cared for. She loves her mother and hopes that her mother will save her. She really, really wants to stop trying so hard. I was originally thinking that these two entities were opposites, but the more time I spend with them, the more I just feel like I need to respect and care for them. They are me."

In the dynamic with her mother, Maria had always felt like she had to fix her mother's dramas, bend to her mother's wishes, and mend her mother's moods. This cycle had depended on Maria being the Hero and her mother being the Victim. To break this cycle, Maria's work would entail reclaiming and owning her own wounds as well as the heroic pieces. By doing this work personally, she would automatically begin to apply it to those around her. Over time, Maria would learn that everyone in her life, including her mother, had their own inner hero. She would learn that it wasn't her job to be a full-time rescuer, nor was anyone a full-time victim. Maria would learn how to sit back, honor her own needs, and see other people as being capable of caring for themselves. This didn't mean that she stopped caring for people; it simply meant that she cared from a place of seeing those around her as equals rather than people who needed to be saved.

Real Stories: Kate

Kate was at a crossroads with her career and needed to find the impetus to apply for a highly competitive position. She had spent the past decade in academia, working through several degrees, yet she never quite felt like she belonged. A shy woman, she had buried herself in books and felt safest when she observed life from the sidelines. She spoke softly, chose her words carefully, and had a habit of putting her hand over her mouth any time she answered a question. She wanted to feel competent at her job and good enough to apply for the new position, yet she constantly second-guessed herself. She shared, "The only thing I've ever been good at is school, but now that I'm surrounded by other academics, I don't feel like I have anything to offer. I never feel smart enough. I never feel like I have enough experience. My colleagues are bold and courageous and seem to have an easier time promoting themselves. I just feel invisible and paralyzed."

She said that her family's primary unwritten rule was that you were supposed to be smart. In her family, "smart" meant everything good—it meant polished, well dressed, and reserved. She had been raised to value grades over peace of mind, multiple degrees over creative pursuits, and rational discussions over emotional intimacy. She said, "It was easy to name the characteristic that went with this rule. Being intellectually competitive was the best way to fit in and to feel loved in my family. My sister was the golden child, always winning awards, always recognized for her achievements. Her nickname was Brainiac, and it feels correct to use her nickname for this aspect because I always wanted to be just like her. However, finding the counterpart was more difficult. At first, I thought maybe I should call her Ignoramus, but that wasn't quite it because it didn't include that feeling of competition. In my family, the worst thing wasn't being stupid or ignorant. No, the worst thing that could possibly happen was being proven wrong when you thought you were right, being a fool, and embarrassing yourself."

This is why it's so important to look at your own history, your family's unwritten rules, and the culture that formed you when you consider naming specific aspects. This work is about searching in the dark for what's been lost, and often deep in that shadow, you'll land on a word, a name, a quality that has a particularly sharp charge, a spark of shame, or a feeling of heavy toxicity. These qualities tend to hold the greatest potential of liberation, although they may require a bit of extra work to get there.

Kate had spent most of her life trying to become the Brainiac in hopes of finally feeling worthy. However, worthiness doesn't work that way. Worthiness isn't found in IQ points, more degrees, achievements, or better grades. Worthiness is experienced by accepting and celebrating exactly who you are. In Kate's case, this would mean not only reclaiming the Brainiac but also reclaiming the thing she never wanted to be, the entity that she named the Fool.

I explained this to her and asked, "Can you take a moment and allow yourself to step into the shoes of the Fool? Think about who she is and what she feels. She's a part of you, and she holds valuable information for you."

Kate shook her head. "I don't want to be a fool. I don't want to identify with it in any way."

I explained, "This isn't really about becoming a fool. It's about allowing yourself the generosity to be a fool sometimes. Instead of trying so hard to never be one, it's more about just allowing yourself to be human, to be complicated, to be an assortment of characteristics. This isn't necessarily about thinking that being a fool is a great thing. It's more about seeing that the Brainiac has good and bad aspects. She's great at some things and terrible at others. On the flip side, the Fool isn't completely bad or completely good. There are great things about being a fool and not so great things about being a fool. This work is to neutralize both sides so that you don't have so much inner resistance to one side or another. It's about relieving the pressure. It's about forgiving yourself and accepting yourself—all aspects of yourself. So can you imagine simply having a conversation with this aspect, the one called the Fool? Could you, just for a moment, ask this part of you who she is and what she feels?"

Katie took a few breaths and nodded slowly before she spoke. "She's very little, maybe four or five. She can't read yet, and she feels embarrassed because her sister, my sister, could already read."

"And what does that little girl, that part of you, need?"

"She needs people to be patient with her. I don't know what else she needs. It just seems like people are impatient with her and she can't keep up."

"And what does that little part of you love?"

"She loves being alone. She loves her cat. She loves drawing pictures," Kate said.

"And what does she really want?" I asked.

"She really wants to have fun. She doesn't want to have to work so hard. She wants to goof off and do things for no reason at all."

"How does it feel to hear those answers?"

"I thought I would hate the answers. I guess that's why I avoided doing this part of the assignment. But I guess, if you're honest and just do the work, it's really profound to simply allow that part of you to speak. I would never have thought that I'd be ever be willing to call myself a fool, but now the word doesn't seem to have any weight to it."

Even though Kate had so much resistance to reclaiming the part of her that she called the Fool, she was profoundly affected by the answers she found. This didn't mean that she had to give up her academic pursuits or her love of learning. In fact, it didn't mean that she had to give up anything at all. Worthy work isn't about becoming a smaller footprint of yourself. It's about widening your perspective, broadening how you define yourself, and having benevolence for all aspects of yourself.

Before this work, Kate felt like an impostor in her field, never quite living up to the idea of who she thought she should be. However, by finding compassion and kindness for the part of her who felt like the Fool, she softened her perspective. Instead of seeing the Brainiac as the most esteemed part of herself and the Fool as something that had to be hidden and denied, she now saw them both as innocent parts of herself that deserved kindness and care.

YOUR WORTHY WORK: Entity Pairs

Now it's your turn. Look over your list of entities, and choose at least three entity pairs. Each pair will include one name who was exiled and the corresponding name who remained. You're looking for any that feel like they have a particular emotional charge—positive or negative.

Take a moment and imagine having a conversation with a specific named entity. For each entity, you will say their name. As you say their name, imagine this entity as a person, a friend, a part of you who was exiled to protect you from suffering, or a part of you who remained behind to try to help you. No matter which side of the wall this entity fell on, when you say their name, have compassion, respect, and reverence for them. And then when you're ready, you will welcome them into the village of you. Close your eyes, picture her in your mind, and take the time to really listen for the answers that arise from within you.

Ask her:

- *Who are you?*
- *What do you feel?*
- *What do you need?*
- *What do you love?*
- *What do you really want?*

This isn't about taking action quite yet; it's about the practice of inquiry. Treat this like a meditation. Take your time with each question. Notice if you find yourself wanting to skip one. Notice if you feel the need to defend, justify, or resist the inquiry process. That is normal. Hold the entity in your mind, and simply ask the questions. Be curious about the nature of each aspect and its influence over you. Hold each idea loosely, and imagine you have the power to have a conversation, have compassion, and welcome this part of you back home.

JOURNAL PROMPTS

1. Think of a time when you felt irrationally triggered or overly emotional. What feelings were present? What part of you was threatened? See if you can find the connection between that experience and your lost self.

2. Which entities seem to be the most difficult or threatening for you? Why do you think they hold such an emotional charge?

3. Think of an example of some aspect or entity who you hoped to avoid, only to have it persist. Why did avoiding this aspect end up backfiring?

CHAPTER 4

What Took Its Place

Nature abhors a vacuum, and when it comes to the lost self, this is profoundly true. For every part of you that's been lost, there will always be something, or often someone, that quickly takes its place. When I look back on my childhood, I can pretty easily draw a straight line between each part of myself that I denied and the aspect of my mother that took up the empty space. My identity was malleable, shape-shifting to become whatever she needed. My emotions were eclipsed by her exaggerated volatility and mania. I was blinded to anything other than what she needed and what I thought might make her happy. And while this strategy helped me survive my childhood, it made me quite dysfunctional as an adult.

Healthy relationships are built through intimacy,

vulnerability, and connection between two people. I had lost myself to the point that I had no sense of self. I was simply an empty container waiting to be told what to do. I busied myself with becoming what I thought was needed of me. *Who am I? What do I feel? What do I need, love, and really want?* I had stopped asking myself those questions. Even if I'd asked, I had no access to my own answers. I had been trained to forget myself, and then I filled all the empty space with someone else.

There's a moment that stands out in my memory, one that perfectly demonstrates exactly how lost I'd become to my own self. It was 2009, a couple of days after I filed for divorce from my first husband, and I went out to pick up some groceries and a movie. It was the first awkward trip out in public. I felt like I had a scarlet letter on my chest advertising that I was now broken, damaged, and alone. I remember standing in the produce aisle as if it were the first time I'd ever seen one. The world was full of possibilities, and it was also dauntingly unknown. It was as if I'd lost my map, my understanding of how to navigate, my knowledge about what to do.

There were stacks of bell peppers, yellow and red, piles of broccoli, romaine lettuce, carrots. For seventeen years, I'd known exactly what to buy because I'd known what my husband liked and didn't like. Eventually, we had a daughter, and I knew how to shop for her as well. I knew what she would eat and what she wouldn't touch. But newly divorced, standing in the grocery store, I realized I had no idea what I actually wanted for myself. I remember touching the bell peppers, wondering, *Do I like bell peppers?* I didn't know. They were pretty and they were colorful, piles of crimson and tangerine and gold. They smelled like the dirt, rain, and that old pizza place that I'd loved as a kid.

And then I remembered the flower stand. In my postdivorce fantasy, I wanted to be the kind of woman who bought beautiful produce and had fresh flowers on her dining table. But in reality, I'd never bought flowers for myself. And now, standing there in front of the bouquets, I wasn't sure what do. I asked myself, *Do I want flowers? Do I even like them?* I'd never really given it much thought.

Next, I went next door to rent a movie. Standing in front of the new release section, I just felt hollow. Cover by cover, I thumbed through the available movies, knowing exactly what my ex would like and what he would be happy watching. My daughter was easy; anything with a fairy or a princess would do. I had the same feeling as I did with the bell peppers and the flowers. *Did I even want to watch a movie? And if so, how would I know which one to watch?*

At the time, I didn't realize how detrimental it was to be a stranger to myself, nor did I understand how it contributed to my overwhelming feelings of worthlessness. I didn't know that by losing my sense of self, I had devalued myself. I didn't know that to raise my self-worth, I needed to claim, own, and possess more of myself. I was focused on the symptoms—getting a divorce, feeling weighed down by burdensome friendships, untangling myself from the dysfunction of my childhood—as if they were unrelated problems. I didn't see then that they were all the same problem: I didn't know who I was, what I felt, what I needed, loved, or wanted. I didn't think that I deserved time, attention, and energy, and instead, I recklessly spent my time, attention, and energy on others. I didn't know where I ended and where someone else began. My idea of self was porous and moldable. I was agreeable to a fault.

On the surface, this made me likable, kind of like one of those friends that you'd see in a movie or a sitcom. That friend who was always available. The friend who'd get in the car and drive to your house in the middle of night if you were upset. The friend who knew all your secrets and who loved you unconditionally. The friend who would talk on the phone for hours if you were hurting. I would watch your kids, cook you dinner, and offer you a bed in my spare room if you were in a bad spot. I would follow you wherever you went if that was what you wanted me to do. I would admire you and tell you how special you were if that was what you needed.

Without a solid sense of self, I forged friendships quickly and easily. Many of my friendships were fabricated in the span of one evening, one conversation, or even one email. When I say quick, I mean that I could go from barely knowing you to being the perfect sidekick within the span of a weekend. At the time, I didn't see the pattern for what it was. I was a dysfunctional genius at figuring out what other people needed from me and then shape-shifting myself to become exactly that. If you needed a confidant, I would be the best listener. If you were shy and afraid, I would be brave and bold. I'd do whatever you needed me to do and say whatever you needed to hear. I'd be strong when you needed support, and I'd be weak and broken when you needed to be the hero. I'd be funny and entertaining when you needed to laugh.

Of course, this wasn't a conscious calculation, nor was I intentionally trying to deceive anyone. I honestly believed that this was how relationships worked, that love was earned through becoming what someone else needed. In other words, I believed that I was worthy of love, friendship, and belonging only when I erased myself completely.

I couldn't have been more wrong. I didn't know that by erasing myself, I made myself impossible to love. I didn't know that by ignoring myself, I eradicated any remaining vestiges of self-worth. I didn't know that my dysfunctional pattern would never get me what I really wanted. I didn't know that this pattern prevented me from ever feeling connection, intimacy, or belonging. And I definitely didn't know that the pattern kept me feeling worthless. I only knew how to ignore myself for a while, and I blindly followed patterns that I'd learned from childhood. I had no awareness of my lost self, but I was painfully aware of the desperation to find relief from the deep ache of worthlessness.

Looking back, I can see now that the strategy seemed to have a pretty reliable expiration date. After a few years, inexplicably but like clockwork, I'd simply be unable to continue being what someone needed me to be or doing what they needed me to do. I'd get to this point where I just couldn't make myself shape-shift anymore. Instead of being eager to please, I would become filled with resentment. Where I was once welcoming, I would become guarded. Where I was once friendly and charming, I would become reserved and cautious. Where I once was eager, I would now become reluctant.

No matter how hard I'd try to convince myself otherwise, I'd get to the point where I couldn't make myself do the whole rigmarole anymore. It was like a light somewhere inside me would go out, and nothing could flip the switch to turn it back on. Eventually, what once felt like friendship would now feel like the burden of guilt, responsibility, and disappointment. I'd try to fix the problem by giving myself some space. I'd tell myself I only needed a day or two and then I'd be ready to get back to the whole shebang. But days would turn into weeks and then months. No amount of time ever seemed to be able to fix the problem. Eventually, the phone would ring and I wouldn't pick it up. I'd hear texts come through, and I couldn't make myself read them, let alone reply to them. When the long email inevitably arrived in my inbox, I wouldn't even look at it. Delete, silence, block. It always ended the same way: I'd ghost them.

At first, I thought this pattern was simply dumb luck. After a few more failed relationships, I chalked it up to having a broken picker. But after a couple of decades of meeting someone only to end up feeling suffocated, strangled, and smothered, I had to face the truth: this was most likely a me problem, and I needed to get to the bottom of it.

I had to learn that when you lose your sense of self or you give too much of yourself to another person, you experience a real and painful loss that feels like not-enough-ness—the source of unworthiness. I had to learn that what I sensed was the diminishment of self, and that would never create a healthy relationship. I had to learn that while my relationship stories always ended with me as a ghost, they started there too. I had lost my sense of self, so I tried to find myself in someone else. I had no real connection with who I was, so it was impossible to find meaningful connections with anyone else.

At best, my people-pleasing skills would simply run their course. The other person would inevitably give up trying to get to know who I was behind the slippery, compliant veneer. At worst, since I'd been trained to be precisely what my mother needed, it made me a perfect match for people who were exactly like my mother. By being forthright in my willingness to be used, I made myself a ripe candidate for predators, narcissists, and emotional vampires. Before I had any hope of building a lasting sense of self-worth, this pattern needed to stop.

THE DISEASE OF THE LOST SELF

In the previous chapters, we've covered three main ideas. First was why you lost yourself: to help you cope with an unbearable truth. Second was how you lost yourself: through defense mechanisms that exiled aspects of self to your unconscious. And third was what you lost: crucial characteristics and aspects of yourself, including access to who you are, what you feel, and what you want, need, and love.

In this chapter, we are going to look at what took the place of your exiled aspects of self and how detrimental this becomes to your well-being. When you lose your core sense of selfhood, you will begin to search elsewhere for meaning, approval, and identity. Instead of seeing yourself as a whole, separate, and contained self, you begin to look to external cues to define you.

> **The more you lose yourself, the more susceptible you are to allowing someone to take over the empty space left behind.**

This exposes you to being controlled, manipulated, and harmed by yourself and others. This dynamic is at the heart of codependency—the disease of the lost self.

Codependency can be defined in many ways. It can be a term used to refer to relationship addiction. It can be a diagnostic term used to describe a chemically dependent individual's partner. In common vernacular, the word may be used to describe someone as weak, needy, or clingy. While these definitions might be applicable in some cases, they merely point to symptoms without defining the underlying problem—a chronic and devastating loss of self.

> **For the purposes of this book, I'll define codependency as the condition of someone else taking the place of your lost self.**

This means that instead of having a solid sense of self, where there's a stable axis running right through your own unique center, you have a flimsy or permeable sense of self that orbits around someone else's axis. This means that while you might not be able to answer these questions—Who are you? What do you feel? What do you need? What do you love? What do you really want?—for yourself, you could easily answer them for the other person. It also means that when you're not answering these questions for yourself, you are rendered vulnerable to those who are willing to answer them for you. This exposes you to having someone else define your identity, your emotions, your needs, and your wants. This causes an incredibly painful and dysfunctional dynamic that makes a healthy relationship impossible. This loss of selfhood leads to a pattern of compulsive behaviors and painful dependence on the approval of others to find safety, self-worth, and identity. If worthiness is the quality of deserving attention, energy, and respect, then codependency is the opposite. It diminishes self-worth by inflating the worth of those around you.

While there is no specific diagnostic for codependency, here are some of the most common warning signs to look for:

- *Trouble articulating and sharing your feelings and beliefs*
- *An insatiable need to be liked or appreciated*
- *An exaggerated sense of responsibility*
- *Feeling guilty for asserting yourself*
- *Trouble with intimacy and boundaries*
- *Chronically prioritizing others over yourself*
- *Ignoring or denying problems in a relationship*
- *A deep-seated lack of self-worth*

All these symptoms point to the same underlying problem: you've lost your sense of self, and someone else has taken its place.

If you consider my history, you can see that I lost access to who I was as a coping mechanism to help me survive childhood abuse, distance myself from my mother's mental illness, and cope with unbearable physical and emotional experiences. However, this loss of self continued into adulthood, setting me up for decades of dysfunctional relationships. Instead of knowing who I was, what I felt, and what I needed, loved, and wanted, I only knew the answers of those around me. This dynamic was at the heart of my failed marriage, failed relationships, and failed friendships. I did this dysfunctional dance with my daughter. Hell, I even did this dance with my dog.

I had no ability to honor or communicate my own feelings. I felt an exaggerated and irrational responsibility for others. I was reckless with myself in hopes of being loved in return. I felt guilty all the time and believed that asserting myself was morally wrong. I stayed quiet when I should have spoken up. Where I'd thought that being compliant and agreeable was a virtue, it always eventually led to an unbearable feeling of resentment. I created situations where I became captive to those around me. And while some may have had malevolent intentions, I can pretty much guarantee that my dog, a little ten-pound Maltipoo named BeeBee, had no intention of doing me harm. It was a me problem. I was an empty shell willing to be told who I was, what I felt, what I needed to do, and what I was worth. I was an empty vessel just hoping to belong.

> **The dysfunctional pattern of codependency never leads to a happy ending.**

When you're not able to articulate your feelings, advocate for your own needs, share your true desires, or communicate clear boundaries, you will inevitably end up where there is no more self to give. Where there is no more self you can offer. Where there is no more self to spare. You inevitably come to the end of the road, where you must surrender yourself completely or save yourself in the only way you know how. You either succumb to annihilation, or you leave, stonewall, ghost, and run.

EMOTIONAL VAMPIRES

In folklore, vampires are undead beings that survive by sucking the blood out of people. Similarly, emotional vampires are people who seem to survive by metaphorically sucking the life force out of other people.[1] Emotional vampires are not exclusively bad people, nor do they always have malevolent intentions. Of course, some can be abusive, vindictive, mean, and cruel. Some emotional vampires might be straight up psychopaths or sociopaths, while others may have clinical personality disorders—antisocial, narcissistic, histrionic, borderline, obsessive compulsive, or dependent personality disorders. However, a large percentage of them are simply highly insecure people attempting to get love in unhealthy and immature ways.

For our work here, the term "emotional vampire" isn't a scientific diagnosis of a particular type of person. Rather, the term is meant to define a particular role within a dysfunctional dynamic. This means that an emotional vampire needs a willing participant. If you resonated with any or all of the characteristics of codependency, you've probably inadvertently become the willing participant with your fair share of emotional vampires.

> **The more you've lost yourself, the more empty space there is for someone else to possess.**

This means that the more you've lost yourself, the more you've unconsciously opened yourself to participate in this dynamic.

While emotional vampires and codependents are often attracted to one another, they aren't exactly polar opposites. While it may seem plausible that codependents fall prey or victim to emotional vampires, this oversimplification neglects a core truth: both lack a healthy sense of self.

> **Both codependents and emotional vampires struggle with an undefined self.**

Neither really know who they are, what they feel, or what they need, love, or want. Both put an exaggerated importance on other people's opinions of them. They both lack a stable sense of self, an inner axis that defines them.

Codependents and emotional vampires share the same goal. They both rely excessively on others to define their identity and help them feel loved and important. Both are unconsciously trying to find their lost self in another person. However, they have different strategies to achieve that goal. A codependent gives away their attention, energy, and respect to boost their sense of self, while the emotional vampire takes someone else's attention, energy, and respect to boost their sense of self.

At the beginning of a relationship, emotional vampires often appear to be bright, talented, charming, and charismatic. In most ways, these people are indistinguishable from anyone else. That is until you break one of their rules. As long as you go along with their narrative, unquestionably submit to their authority, take the blame, maintain loyalty at all costs, overlook their tantrums, make them look good, and supply their unending cravings for admiration and power, everything will probably seem fine. They need you to survive, so your noncompliance threatens their very existence. Like a fly in the spider's web, you won't know that you are prey until you try to get free, and by then, it's too late. The dysfunctional dynamic has allowed them to fester into wounded victims, grandiose martyrs, controlling guilt trippers, and melodramatic attention hogs.

Whether they do so intentionally or not, emotional vampires constantly seek your attention and drain your energy by demanding your time, energy, and care. They often take advantage of your vulnerabilities and use them to manipulate you for their own benefit. They inflate how they feel about themselves by making you feel worse about yourself. They hold you responsible for supplying their unending need for approval, appreciation, and self-worth. And then they leave you feeling like you've done something wrong, feeling less than and disrespected. Emotional vampires are people who draw you in and then suck you dry, leaving you feeling overwhelmed, depressed, defensive, angry, and exhausted.

Since it's impossible to know what someone else is thinking

or feeling, it is difficult to discern whether someone is an emotional vampire. However, it is much more helpful to consider your own experience to determine whether you're falling into common traps set by emotional vampires. Here are some warning signs to look for:

- *Their feelings, needs, and desires seem more important than yours.*
- *Problems within the relationship feel like they are all your fault.*
- *You feel crazy, like your experiences and reactions don't make any sense.*
- *You feel guilty for not being or doing what they want.*
- *You don't feel like you have permission to have privacy or boundaries.*
- *You don't feel safe showing vulnerability.*
- *You have a difficult time setting boundaries.*
- *Acceptance feels conditional.*
- *There is comparison and competition rather than cooperation.*
- *You feel like a possession rather than a friend or partner.*
- *You feel responsible for stabilizing their tantrums.*
- *You feel like no amount of praise, gratitude, admiration, or appreciation will ever satisfy them.*

Regardless of the symptom, the behavior will point to the same underlying problem: they have abandoned themselves in hopes of laying claim to you.

It's important to note that in one relationship, someone might act like a codependent, and in another, they might act like an emotional vampire. When I look back on my relationship history, there are relationships where I played the role of emotional vampire, even though I didn't mean to. And there are relationships where I played the role of codependent, even though I tried not to. You may find that you have fallen into one or both of these patterns as well. It's not right or wrong. It's simply what happens when two people are lost: both participants suffer.

The good news is that there is a way out of this dynamic, one that fortifies you against participating in dysfunction, prevents emotional vampires from ever laying claim to you, and stops you from losing yourself in another person. The answer is boundaries.

SETTING BOUNDARIES

Maybe your boundaries have been strong enough to protect you from emotional vampires and keep you out of the muck of codependency. However, for every part of you that's been lost, there's an empty space left open to be occupied. So before you can fully reclaim your lost self, you will need to evict whatever or whomever has taken residence in place of your lost self. This means that you need strong boundaries if you want to repossess the self that's rightfully yours.

> **Boundaries are crucial to the process of reclaiming your lost self, and they are also the cornerstone of healthy relationships.**

When you have healthy boundaries, you are able to show up as a whole self, experience true intimacy with others, and enjoy a sense of freedom in every relationship. When you have unhealthy boundaries, you can feel stuck, helpless, over-whelmed, and resentful.

You may not need to change every relationship. However, you need better boundaries in any relationship that has any of the follow symptoms:

- *You often feel frustrated or angry after interactions with the person.*
- *You feel like you're walking on eggshells around the person.*
- *You bend over backward to avoid letting the person down.*
- *You feel like you are doing something wrong.*
- *You feel like you're going to be outcast or unloved if you're not doing what the person wants.*

- *You're often exhausted after engaging with the person.*
- *You tend to give away too much of your time and energy to the person.*
- *You say yes to things you don't want to do.*
- *You feel like the person wants to control, change, or dominate you.*
- *You often find yourself oversharing personal and private information with the person.*
- *You avoid making clear plans with the person and prefer to leave things ambiguous.*
- *You feel responsible for the person's feelings, thoughts, or actions.*
- *You have a difficult time finding your center when you're around the person.*

To strengthen boundaries, it's important to understand what they are and what they are not.

> **The definition of a boundary is a line that marks the limits of an area; it's both a line of containment (keeping you in) and a line of protection (keeping others out).**

Think about this like drawing a circle around yourself. Inside the circle is your mental, emotional, physical, and spiritual space. This space is where you live. It is the space that your whole self occupies. It includes all the aspects of yourself that you love, cherish, and celebrate. It also includes all the aspects of yourself that you have forgotten, denied, and repressed. No one else belongs in that circle. You can't reclaim this space if you're sharing it with someone else. This means that anyone occupying the space inside your circle must move outside the line. It also means that you need to stay within your own circle and refrain from bleeding outside the lines and into someone else's circle.

Boundaries are not complaints, threats, or ultimatums. They are not manipulation. They aren't mean, cruel, or rude. Boundaries are guidelines—tangible or intangible limits—that help clearly define what needs to be protected.

> **Boundaries are your rules for who, what, how, and why you feel comfortable being close to someone else, clear communication of what's true for you, helping others know who you are and how to interact with you.**

When you are clear with your boundaries, no one around you is left guessing.

Worthiness is built on a foundation of healthy boundaries because healthy boundaries start with honoring, respecting, and caring for yourself. To do this, you must clearly define what will be sustainable for you. This means that you figure out what will support you, what will sustain you, and what will stop your resources from becoming depleted.

There are two common misunderstandings when it comes to the topic of healthy boundaries. The first is that you might mistakenly confuse offering instructions or telling someone what to do with setting a boundary. Instructions are guidelines given to someone in an attempt to influence them or their behavior. Boundaries are not about the other person; they are about you. They are not about a command or consequences. They are about sharing how you operate, what's true for you, and what works for you. They are about making a request and waiting for feedback. The person may or may not honor your request. No matter what course of action the person takes, their behavior is crucial feedback. If they honor your request, it will likely create calm within the relationship, a sense of equality and balance. If they ignore your request, it's up to you to take the necessary actions to protect and restore your boundary. This means that you remove yourself from a situation, leave the party, shut a door, hang up, or do what's needed to create the boundary yourself.

For example, instead of complaining that someone keeps calling too late, you'd communicate, "I turn my phone off after

8:00 p.m." Instead of policing their behavior, you'd simply turn your phone to do-not-disturb mode so you're not bothered. You change your behavior to create the boundary rather than wait for the other person to honor your request.

When you're trying to set clear boundaries, a simple yes, no, or thank you works wonders. When someone does something that breaches your boundary, say something like, "That doesn't work for me," or "That doesn't feel good to me." If someone repeatedly tries to contact you, you can say, "Please do not call/text/email/show up again." If (when) they do it again, unfollow, unfriend, block their phone number or their social media access to you, or set up an email filter to protect your valuable space, time, and energy.

When someone violates a boundary, start by clearly stating your request. A request focuses on what you want rather than putting the focus on what you don't want. A possible request script is "I would like [fill in the blank]." Or "I would appreciate [fill in the blank]." (Keep it very simple. The fewer words the better.)

The second misunderstanding about healthy boundaries is that you might mistakenly believe that a boundary creates conflict, separation, distance, or disconnection in a relationship. You might believe that if you share your truth or honor your core desires, you'll be cast out or cut off from the ones you love. To avoid this, you might want to avoid setting boundaries altogether. But this is exactly how the line between you and others becomes blurred. If you don't check in with yourself first and become clear on your own individual truth, you'll unintentionally connect with others in disingenuous ways.

> **When you don't clearly communicate who you are, you foster inauthentic relationships that lack true connection.**

A healthy boundary honors the truth about who you are, what you feel, what you need, and what you desire. A healthy boundary helps you communicate who you are to yourself and to others. Therefore, boundaries are not the opposite of intimacy; rather, they create intimacy by authentically communicating intimate information with those around you. The more meaningful the relationship, the more important it is to communicate and honor boundaries. Healthy relationships grow with the understanding that each person within that relationship deserves to set their own limits and ask clearly for what they want and do not want. Healthy boundaries bring you closer to people who respect you while keeping your sense of self intact.

TAKING BACK WHAT'S YOURS

Anger is an important and necessary emotion, and it is critical for reclaiming your lost self and for strengthening your sense of self-worth. It is the natural and appropriate emotional response to boundary violations and unfairness. Anger comes in many flavors, from irritation, impatience, and annoyance to wrath, exasperation, fury, and resentment. Healthy anger rises up in proportionate intensity to the threat or infraction. Whether someone (or something) has encroached on your boundary or something has become increasingly unfair, anger ensures that you fight, hold your ground, and protect what's yours. Anger signals that a boundary has been violated and asks for you to protect where the breach occurred.

Before you can fully reclaim the parts of you that you've denied, pushed away, and forgotten, you must first repossess any part of your personal territory that has been claimed by someone else. This means that anyone who inhibits your ability to know who you are, what you feel, what you need, what you love, and what you want can no longer occupy the space inside your personal boundary circle. This also means that any time you've prioritized another person's identity, feelings, needs, and wants, you must bring yourself back inside your personal boundary circle.

This step is paying attention to when and where and why you feel angry, frustrated, or protective. This first means that you need to give yourself permission to privately feel, honor, and express anger toward someone or something. This work is solely for you; nothing needs to be expressed to anyone else for you to take back what's rightfully yours. This work is about becoming aware of your mental, emotional, physical, and spiritual boundary circle and noticing the irritation, aggravation, or general pissed-off-ness that you feel when someone else tries to lay claim within your rightful territory.

Please take your time with this. This work is intentional and thoughtful. This step is about repossessing ownership of your whole self. It's about clearly defining the line around you so that it's occupied by you and only you. Take an inventory of your relationships. Pay special attention to any relationships that feel taxing, draining, or exhausting. Notice any symptoms that relate to codependency, emotional vampires, or blurry boundaries.

For each of these relationships, ask yourself: *When do I feel frustration, irritation, and anger in this relationship? What triggered the anger? What boundary was breached? What course of action is necessary for me to restore my boundary?*

This doesn't mean that you don't care about the person or that you no longer want to have a relationship with that person. In fact, this is the best way to create meaningful connections and sustainable relationships with those around you. It's also important to note that it's easier to consider strengthening boundaries in some areas more than others.

It's common to find an inner resistance to doing boundary work. That is normal and to be expected. Boundaries are difficult, and they take time and practice. In the next chapter, you'll take this work further to reclaim and celebrate what's been lost. But for now, the work is simply to eliminate anyone or anything that has taken up residence in place of your lost self. To give you a better idea of how this works, let me share a few examples.

WHAT TOOK ITS PLACE

Real Stories: Elena

Elena wanted to create a life beyond motherhood. As a single mother of a teenage son, she was eager for him to go to college but nervous about the approaching empty nest. For nearly twenty years, her life had revolved around him in every way. Now, as she looked to her future, she felt unsure about who she was or what life would be without her son at home. When it came to answering questions in class, she could easily answer for her son. She knew who he was, what he felt, what he needed, but she was at a loss when it came to finding the answers for herself. She shared, "I poured myself into motherhood, and I loved every bit of it. I was a good mom, and I'm proud of that. But now it's time to make myself a priority. My son has his whole life out in front of him. And I want to be happy for him, but I am worried. I feel lost. I don't know who I am or what to be excited about. And I don't want to end up as a sad, empty shell of a woman without a sense of purpose."

She was reluctant to share her homework. She said that she felt disloyal and guilty and didn't want to give the wrong impression about her son. While she knew she needed help with the work, she was very concerned that her work would reflect poorly on him. She said, "When I reviewed all my relationships, I just kept coming back to my son. You said to look for irritation or anger or feeling exhausted, and I hate to admit that this might be the case with my son. I love him and he's wonderful, but I am constantly annoyed with him. He's a teenager, and he pushes my buttons, and then I feel guilty for being mad. I don't want to think that he's an emotional vampire. That sounds terrible. I just can't go there."

Although Elena was aware of her irritation, she was unaware of what was causing it. And it's understandable why she might not want to look at the most meaningful relationship in her life with a critical eye. However, boundary problems are created by you, not by the other person. This means that when you have boundary problems, you can easily turn a completely innocent person into something that resembles an emotional vampire. So while it felt disloyal to share her frustration about her son, the work wasn't about him. It was about Elena. She had lost herself in her son and seemed to be in a codependent dynamic with him. Even the way she tried to manage the image of her son and felt guilty about sharing her work about him pointed back to prioritizing him over herself. Most likely, her son didn't want this from her. Most teenagers are busy differentiating themselves from their parents and doing their own work to find themselves. Elena would need to do this work herself. She'd need to clearly define herself so that she saw her son as a whole and separate entity. Anger happens in response to boundary violations. My hunch was that her irritation wasn't caused by her son but rather from Elena violating her own boundaries.

I explained this to her and asked, "Do you know what typically triggers the anger?"

She said, "I can't put my finger on it. It seems like I'm always irritated or like I'm always tired. He stays up so late at night, and I'm a zombie at that hour."

"If you're a zombie at that hour, why are you awake?"

"Well, he's leaving for college in a few months, and I don't want to miss anything. So I stay up late with him just in case he needs help with homework or to keep him company. The problem is that I still have to wake up at the crack of dawn to get my work done. So I drink more coffee and get less sleep. It's a vicious cycle. I don't know what else to do though."

This is a common misunderstanding when you are a kind and compassionate person. Elena cared about her son, and her love for him was obvious. However, she was sacrificing her own needs in the name of "care and kindness." By forgoing her own need for sleep, she was making herself a martyr. Rather than keeping her center axis within her own circle, she was orbiting around her son. My hunch was that he wasn't even asking her to do this. Therefore, she was not only crossing her own boundary by prioritizing him over herself, but it was also possible that she was crossing his boundary.

I explained this to her and said, "This may not be what you want to admit, but it's important to look at where the anger is coming from. Why do you think you feel irritated?"

Elena took a moment to think before her eyes widened with shock. "I think I'm angry because he's not grateful for my sacrifices. Like, I want him to notice that I'm giving up my sleep for him. Oh no, that's not good."

"It's not good and it's not bad. It's simply a matter of having blurry boundaries and operating within a codependent dynamic. However, the good news is that your irritation is giving you clear direction as to where you need to strengthen your boundaries. Rather than martyring yourself and then being angry that you're not appreciated, your work will be to honor yourself and care for your own needs. What boundary needs to be set by you for you?" I asked.

"Well, for starters, I guess I need to take responsibility for my own sleep."

Before Elena could begin to fully reclaim her lost self, she would need to stop her habit of focusing exclusively on her son. This wouldn't mean that she would stop loving him or stop caring for him. Rather, it would mean that instead of seeing him as the center of her life, she'd need to begin to create a life where she was at the center. By having clear boundaries for herself, her son would no longer feel burdened or responsible for her needs, wants, and feelings. Likewise, she would feel free to care about and honor her own needs. This would not only offer her son the space and freedom to launch into his new life but would also help Elena focus on the life she wanted to create.

Real Stories: Jasmine

Jasmine wanted to find some motivation and inspiration. She had moved to a new town the previous year, hoping to bring some excitement and vitality to her life. Yet the move had only made things worse. Instead of taking steps to invest in her community, she'd become more of a homebody, and now her life revolved around her two small dogs, television, and junk food. She was content with her daily routine; she walked her dogs twice a day in her neighborhood, got coffee at the shop on the corner, and waved hello to anyone she passed on the street. Yet it all felt meaningless to her; her life had become complacent and boring. She said ever since she retired, she had felt drab and lackluster. Her extended family now lived on the opposite coast and only visited at the holidays, she had a few friends but rarely saw them, and her pension covered her humble expenses. She shared, "I am lonely but unmotivated to go out and meet people. I am bored but not disciplined enough to make myself do something. I feel like my life is getting smaller, and I don't know how to make myself change. I keep falling back on junk food and TV."

When Jasmine shared her homework, she said that she lived alone and wasn't sure that she had any work to do in this category other than being helplessly codependent with her dogs. Since she had no close relationships and was alone most of the time, she didn't think she would find any boundary work to do. Yet she was determined to do all the course homework, so she focused on her emotions, specifically looking for signs of anger, frustration, and irritation.

Within the first couple of days, she was astonished to find an unsettling amount of anger seething under the surface of almost every waking moment. When she tried to pinpoint where the anger was coming from, she found that it wasn't about any of her current relationships. She wasn't angry at her kids, her dogs, or her friends. However, she was shocked to find a deep reservoir of rage for her mother, but she wasn't sure if she was doing the exercise right because her mother wasn't part of her life at all. In fact, she had been dead for twenty-five years. Nonetheless, Jasmine realized how often she was replaying scenes from her childhood, mentally arguing with her mother, revising history, and playing out scenes of revenge in her mind. She said, "Now that I'm paying attention, it's embarrassing to recognize that I'm living out my lonely days having imaginary arguments with my dead mother like a crazy person. You said to look for anger. And boy, did I find it. The more I think about it, the more I see that my mom was an emotional vampire. She sucked me dry while she was alive, and here I am twenty-five years later, still bleeding out."

Anger helps protect. It gives you your life force, and it pumps blood to your extremities so that you can fight. It fills you with fire and lights your fury. It is vital to survival. When you repress your anger or dissociate from it, you lose your strength, stamina, and spunk. Without anger, you don't have the sense of urgency to protect yourself, and you stop fighting for yourself. You become stagnant, apathetic, and boring. You lose your mojo, your creativity, and your motivation.

Somewhere along the line, this is exactly what had happened to Jasmine. She'd lost her spark and become complacent in an uninspired hamster wheel of a life. Jasmine's ongoing apathy and unacknowledged rage pointed to a severe boundary issue. Boundaries aren't only necessary for people within your immediate circle; they are also important for anyone who occupies your inner space. This can include distant family, old friends, social media trolls, or people who you've never even met. Anyone who occupies your mental, emotional, physical, or spiritual space needs to move outside your circle. Even though her mother was long gone, she was alive and well in Jasmine's personal space.

For this reason, Jasmine desperately needed stronger boundaries. Before she could reclaim her lost self, she would need to remove her mother for good.

I explained this to her and said, "I realize that your mother isn't intentionally violating your boundaries anymore, and even though she's been gone for twenty-five years, she's still occupying a tremendous amount of mental real estate right now. What boundary do you think you need to set?"

Jasmine thought for a moment and then responded, "Well, I need to get her out of my head. I need to stop having these stupid arguments with her. I need to stop being angry at her."

"Yes and no. You do need to stop having the mental arguments, but you also need to keep the anger. Otherwise, you will go right back to repressing the anger and numbing out to cope with it. That anger is protecting you. It's showing you where the boundary line should be. It's giving you strength to do what's needed here."

Jasmine looked confused and said, "I have no idea what's needed here."

Boundaries are about you; they are not about the other person. And that is never more clear than when you need to set boundaries with someone who isn't even in your life any longer. Jasmine needed to protect her inner experience. To put it simply, she needed to evict her mother and revoke all access to conversations, arguments, scenarios, and mother-related ruminations. This meant she would need to have very firm boundaries with herself and would need to stop herself from mentally engaging with her mother.

I explained this to her and said, "I know your mother was a very important and painful figure in your life, and I am sorry that you are still suffering from what she did and didn't do. However, she doesn't get to live here anymore. She doesn't get to live in your body, in your house, in your head, or in your heart. Those are your rightful property, and you need to protect what's yours. She doesn't get to suck you dry, argue with you, make you feel bad, or take up any more space. You get to move on and fight for your own life. And you are worth fighting for."

Jasmine exhaled and closed her eyes. "Okay, that feels right. But how do I do that?" she asked.

"Imagine drawing a line around yourself. Inside the circle is your energy. It's your life, who you are, what you feel, and what you love. No one gets to be inside the circle but you. Now picture your mother wanting to get inside the circle."

"She wouldn't want to just get inside the circle. She would want to erase it," Jasmine said with a laugh.

"Okay, imagine that she tries to erase the circle. You are the one who owns your boundary, and you are the one who needs to clearly communicate that the line is not hers to erase. This is going to take practice, but instead of going down the rumination rabbit hole, you will clearly state the boundary and revoke her access," I said.

"So I just say, 'You're not welcome here anymore'?" Jasmine asked.

"Imagine saying that right now. How does it feel?" I asked.

Jasmine smiled. "It feels strong. It feels good. I feel lighter, like I just lost fifty pounds."

Boundaries are an ongoing practice. You don't set a boundary once and then hope it sticks. It's an ongoing part of the relationship, whether you're in contact with that person or not. For Jasmine, her work would be to break her mental habit of allowing the old stories to take up space in her mind, her heart, and her life. By eradicating this baggage, her load would be lightened and she'd be free to use her energy for creating a life she really wanted. Where she had been living a small life and spending most of her mental energy spinning in circles, she would now be free to break out of the bondage of her old stories. This wouldn't be a quick fix, but it would start her in the direction of reclaiming her whole self.

Real Stories: Liz

Liz wanted to find the courage to leave her career and start a new business. She had devoted the past ten years to working for a software company, even though her heart was never really in it. Liz had always been a hard worker and prided herself on her work ethic and stamina. However, management made it difficult for her to remain loyal. No matter how much she gave at the office, the demands never stopped. She was continuously being given more responsibility, while her ability to perform was consistently being undermined. She shared, "It's like I'm trying to keep the boat from sinking by bailing out a tiny teaspoon at a time. My manager is so stressed out that he forgets important things and makes mistakes that create so much extra work for me and for my team. I'm busy covering for him and then always apologizing to my team for his mistakes. In the end, everyone is overworked and underappreciated. I am constantly tired, but I can't sleep at night. I don't want to quit while it's all such a mess, but I also can't imagine continuing to do this. I feel helpless and stuck."

She said that the primary relationship where she experienced frustration, irritation, and anger was with her direct supervisor. Although she respected and admired her supervisor, she was exasperated by his inability to give clear and concise directions. She said that she spent an extraordinary amount of energy trying to guess what he wanted and what the company itself needed. Her supervisor was overworked and overstressed and never had time to clearly explain what Liz needed to do. Yet anytime Liz made a mistake, he would explode. Liz said, "I feel like I'm always walking on eggshells, not only trying to figure out what I'm supposed to do but also trying to figure out how to keep a lid on his volatility. I can't do my job, manage my team, and also be responsible for my supervisor's faulty leadership skills. So I know I need to set a boundary, but the only boundary I can think of is to quit my job and start my own company."

This is a common misunderstanding when it comes to setting boundaries. In Liz's case, she felt like she only had two choices: either to be stuck in a dysfunctional work relationship or to quit and leave. The problem with this is that no matter where you go, boundary issues will follow you. Leaving, moving, or quitting does not fix them; it only gives them a new venue.

Liz was a perfect fit for her supervisor's brand of blurry boundaries. Even if she quit her job and started her own company, inevitably she would end up with the same dynamic— perhaps with a client, a vendor, or an employee. Rather than continuing in the pattern or completely quitting, she would need to clearly define the line that separated her from her supervisor. This means that she would need clear communication rather than trying to avoid his volatility. She would have to protect her energy, time, and personal resources rather than overgiving and overworking. She would need to set personal boundaries for when she worked, how long she worked, and how much stress she was willing to shoulder. She would need to learn how to say no.

I explained this to her and asked, "Can you give me an example of a boundary that might need to be in place?"

She nodded. "Yes, an easy one is that I need to stop working on weekends, but if I'm not available on weekends, my boss will lose his mind. He'll start texting me, emailing me, and relentlessly calling me. It's just not worth it."

I said, "I know how overwhelming it can be when you're in this type of dynamic. However, the goal of the boundary isn't to try to change his behavior. It's to change yours. He's allowed to call you night and day. He's allowed to text you a thousand times. It's bizarre and intrusive, but ultimately it's not your job, nor do you have the power, to change his behavior. What you can do, though, is change your own behavior. You set your boundary, and then you take action to protect it. This might mean that you turn your phone off for the weekend, you silence his calls and texts, or you pace in circles and sit on your hands until the compulsion to respond leaves your body. No matter what course of action you come up with, the change and the boundary come from you."

Liz looked at me wide eyed and worried. "I can't even imagine doing that. That is the exact opposite of what I normally do. I don't know that I have the strength nor the courage to stand up to him like that."

I said, "This isn't about standing up to him. It's about standing up for you. Sometimes it's easier to understand boundaries if you imagine the other person as a toddler. Right now, your supervisor wants to be able to contact you whenever it is convenient for him. He wants what he wants when he wants it. And if he doesn't get it, he throws a tantrum, right?"

Liz smiled. "Yes, you could say that. A very scary tantrum, but yes, a tantrum."

"And what do you do when a toddler throws a fit? Give him the toy? Give him the candy?"

"No," Liz said. "You walk away and don't give him attention."

"Yes, that is exactly what you have to learn to do. When grown-ups throw tantrums, it works the same way. You remove your attention and stop fanning the emotional flames. You don't need to be rude or unkind about it at all. Just like with a toddler, don't be mean. Just don't allow yourself to be manipulated," I said.

"So do I need to tell him ahead of time? I don't feel good about just turning my phone off without letting him know," Liz said.

Boundaries are hard, especially when you're new to them. They are about communicating what works for you and how you operate. So it's best to draft a script for yourself ahead of time. Notice if you want to apologize, add extra niceties, or soften the boundary in some way—this knee-jerk reaction is in opposition to the goal. Boundaries aren't about appearing nice; they are about protecting what's rightfully yours. And standing in that power can feel uncomfortable when it's unfamiliar.

The goal is to communicate only what is true, kind, and necessary. When it comes to boundary scripts, the shorter the better. Keep the script as clean as possible, editing out anything other than what needs to be communicated. Try writing up two or three possible scripts, cut anything that isn't necessary, and then use the script that is brief, true, friendly, and firm.

I explained this to Liz and said, "Your script basically needs to state when you are and are not available. So maybe you say something like, 'I am no longer available on weekends. From here on, I will respond to messages on the following business day.' Or maybe you say something like, 'I'll be off the grid on the weekends from here on out. If you need something, please let me know on a weekday.' Regardless of the script, the important action is that you revoke access and protect your space."

As Liz had guessed, her supervisor did not immediately honor her request. It's common for boundary violators to push back, add pressure, and up the ante. This is often called a "change-back attack," where the person is trying to get you to change back to the original dysfunctional pattern. Liz's supervisor grew increasingly agitated and called, texted, and emailed multiple times. But Liz did not cave and did not reply until work hours on the following Monday. She kept her promise and protected her boundary. Surprisingly, by then, he had already figured out what he needed, and the so-called emergency had passed. Her boss did the same thing the following weekend, but this time it was easier for Liz to hold the boundary because she'd learned a valuable lesson. She now knew that she was the only person who would protect, care for, and defend what was rightfully hers. She no longer saw the dynamic as out of her control but rather as something that was solely her responsibility. This did not fix her overall job dissatisfaction, but it did teach her how to end a dysfunctional pattern and how to start protecting herself. This skill was not only valuable for her current job but would be crucial for eventually starting her own business.

YOUR WORTHY WORK: Relationships

Now it's your turn. Take an inventory of your relationships. You're looking for anyone who has filled the empty space of your lost self. Pay special attention to any relationships that feel taxing, draining, or exhausting. Notice if any symptoms relate to codependency, emotional vampires, or blurry boundaries. These do not need to be people who are in your immediate circle. They can be people whom you see every day or people whom you haven't seen in decades.

For each of these relationships, ask yourself: *When do I feel frustration, irritation, and anger in this relationship? What triggered the anger? What boundary was breached? What course of action is necessary for me to restore my boundary?*

Write down what you need to do to protect and restore your own boundaries. Brainstorm as many ideas as possible. This will most often involve an action that you must take to limit or revoke access, protect your well-being, and make space for the life that is rightfully yours. You do not have to follow through if you're not ready. There is still a great amount of value in articulating this step for your own personal understanding.

Please take your time with this. This work is intentional and thoughtful. This step is about repossessing ownership of your whole self. It's about clearly defining the line around you so that it's occupied by you and only you. It's about clearing space around yourself so that you can easily access the answers to the following questions:

- *Who am I?*
- *What do I feel?*
- *What do I need?*
- *What do I love?*
- *What do I really want?*

If anything or anyone hinders your ability to find your own answers, they need to move outside your personal boundary line.

Boundaries are difficult, and they take time and practice. Treat this like a meditation. Take your time with each question. Notice if you find yourself wanting to skip one. Notice if you feel the need to defend, justify, or resist the inquiry process. That is normal.

JOURNAL PROMPTS

1. Reflect on your past and present relationships. Find an example of a relationship where you lost yourself, and write about that experience. What did it feel like? Why did it happen? What have you learned since then?

2. How do you feel about setting boundaries? When is it challenging? When is it easy? How do you typically react, and/or what do you typically do when your boundaries are not honored?

3. Make a list of people you've known who've had clear boundaries. How did it feel to interact with them? Make a list of people you've known who had unclear or messy boundaries. How did it feel to interact with them?

CHAPTER 5

Reclaiming Your Lost Self

Somewhere around my forty-second birthday, after years (decades, really) of striving, doing, trying, I hit a wall. Some call it "burnout." For me, it was more like being reduced to ash. Except I did not rise like the phoenix. I lay down and stayed down. And then life just kept swinging punches, and I couldn't catch my breath. I was physically sick, mentally exhausted, and financially broke. The tip of the iceberg was a massive business failure with hundreds of thousands of dollars lost. Under that was excruciating heartbreak as I watched everything into which I'd poured my energy, time, emotional strength, and all my money evaporate in the span of a few weeks. And then there was an ocean of emails to respond to, events to cancel, refunds to issue, leases to negotiate, lawyers to meet with, doctor's appointments, vet bills to pay, and therapy sessions to keep. But beyond all the physical, financial, heartbreaking vulnerability of it all, I lost a part of myself that I never thought I could lose. I lost hope.

Up until that point, I'd seen my life like an upward vector, always rising, always improving. Hope was a thing that propelled me forward. Hope was a thing that made me want to grow, give, excel. Hope lifted me and gave me direction. It gave life meaning.

To lose hope meant that everything felt arbitrary. Nothing really had meaning. My life was no longer a vector always rising higher. It was a simply a scattering of meaningless dots on a pointless graph. Without hope, there was no significance to my suffering. Without hope, there was no reason for any of it.

I don't know what it was about this specific set of events that leveled me so severely. I had been through hard times before. I'd had my fair share of disillusionment and betrayals. I'd lost plenty of money before. This was definitely not my first failure. But this time, I'd been rocked to the point where any sense of optimism had been nullified. It wasn't that I'd become a full-blown cynic; it was more that I simply felt nothing. Life seemed random and unchangeable. Things were hard and felt like they were going to keep being hard. It seemed like nothing was going to change, so why bother? It felt like my only choice was to surrender to the unchangeability. It was as though I'd finally given the universe permission to do what it does, and I vowed to stop spending my time and energy falsely believing that I could change any of it.

This wasn't exactly a conscious decision, but it did feel justified. At that point, hope felt naive, immature, and reckless. At the time, by giving up hope, I believed I was choosing a more rational, intelligent, and mature strategy. I lost hope because keeping it became too painful. It might seem counterintuitive that something positive would be surrendered to ease suffering, so let me explain.

The lost self isn't comprised of only negative traits. You can lose access to both the dark and the light parts of yourself. Both can be threatening. Both can put you at risk. And both can be hidden from your awareness.

Even though hope would be labeled a positive trait for many, for me, it became burdened with its own set of liabilities. Namely, it put me at risk for disappointment. To have hope meant that I had expectations for the future. It meant that I had ideas about what could happen, wishes for what I wanted to have happen, and the belief that I had the ability to influence the circumstances of my life. For hope to exist, change had to feel possible. When change no longer felt possible and I felt like I no longer had any sense of agency over my future, hope became impossible to hold on to.

Up until then, change had always felt possible. Not only possible, it had felt inevitable. Even in the darkest moments of my childhood, I knew I would eventually grow up and be able to move out of my parents' home. I knew that at some point, I would no longer be at the mercy of their cruelty. During the darkest hours of my divorce, I knew eventually my heart would heal over. And even when I was flat broke, I was able to maintain the belief that a better financial future was merely few good ideas away.

Yet amid the business failures, worsening physical ailments, and chaos that encompassed my life that year, the reality of disappointment began to outweigh the possibility of change. Maybe it was because I'd had my heart broken too many times. Maybe it was because I'd been physically sick for too long. Maybe it was because I'd started doubting that I'd ever really recover from the legacy of my childhood. Or maybe it was because I was just too damned tired to care anymore.

Somewhere around that time, I remember driving up the coast. It was one of those days where the sun sparkled gold across the water. Everything was gold and blue, the sky, the clouds, the sea. I remember thinking that a scene like that could almost make you believe that anything was possible. And that was when I realized how guarded I felt. Before that moment, I hadn't realized that I was physically holding myself as if I were in danger. And the danger oddly seemed to be related to the experience of joy, well-being, or the idea of open possibilities. It was as if I was afraid to let myself feel good.

I tried to relax, but my body was stiff and barely breathing, as if a deep inhale would break me wide open. As if the beauty of this moment might hurt me beyond repair. I couldn't let it in, the brilliance of the light, the gravity of the moment, the infinite possibility of joy. Like trying to stare at the sun, it felt dangerous, and I wanted to shield myself from it. And if I did let it in, for even a breath, I was sure that it would immediately destroy me.

To be clear, it wasn't that I had lost the ability to see good in the world. I never stopped loving my daughter. I never stopped taking care of my dog. I still bought groceries and cooked dinner and watched movies, just like I always had. I went for walks and watched the sunset and read poetry. I still felt compassion for those who suffered around me. I just stopped believing I could do anything about it. I stopped believing I could influence or change it. But it wasn't until that moment in the car, when I realized I was bracing myself against the magnificence of that moment, that I realized I'd lost something profound, something deeply necessary, but I wasn't yet able to name it.

During the course of that year, I was aware of having lost an important part of me, but I didn't quite know what had been lost. It was as if this part of me was hidden just outside my peripheral vision. I knew something in me had been relegated to the shadow, but every time I tried to name the aspect or to focus on it, I'd lose sight of it. Months later, I took myself back to that car ride again and again and tried to articulate what it was that I had felt and what exactly I had lost. What had I come up against in the car, the shielding against joy, the holding myself rigid against possibilities, the unwillingness to feel the vulnerability of the moment? It felt related to God, to prayer, to faith. It felt related to magic, to making wishes, to wide-open imagination. I searched my memories and combed through my experiences, wanting to give a name to the aspect I'd lost. The best way I could explain it to myself was that I'd lost the belief that things would eventually turn out okay, that things might get better. I'd lost access to the sacred, the spiritual, the mystical. In the end, I called this lost part of me "hope" and continue to do so here for simplicity's sake, but in reality, it was more complicated, more painful, and more intricate than one word could describe. What I'd lost was a combination of trust, faith, hope, and joy.

My next step was to neutralize what I'd come to call hope. This required me to remember who I had been before any of this. I needed to trace my history back to the little me who had been willing to trust, effortlessly joyful, and full of belief in open possibilities. When I charted the path back to my memories of hope, one stood out stronger than the rest. I remembered being a little girl, lying in bed trying to fall asleep. Summers in my hometown were hot and dead still. My house was a mountain range away from any hint of coastal breeze, surrounded by blond grasslands rolling over the hills for as far as the eyes could see. More than anything, I remembered what the summer night sounded like. I remembered how I would move my pillow to the foot of my bed and position myself just under the window. That was the only place in my bedroom where I could see a slice of the starry sky. That was when I would listen. I didn't know the sound came from crickets. To me, the stars were singing, each pinpoint in chorus with the others, each song a message for me. I felt held, seen. I could hear them, and in turn I believed they could hear me too. The song was the magic of the sky, and I heard it because I believed I had magic in me too.

When I looked back on the little me who used to believe she could hear the stars, I remembered the girl who needed hope more than anything. When I asked myself who she was, what she felt, what she needed, loved, and wanted, it snapped me viscerally back into my old self, the bedroom, the childhood, the sound of the night. When I thought of that little girl looking up at the stars, I realized I would never be so cruel as to take away her hope. I would never want her to feel helpless or powerless. That little me was a girl who needed to believe things would change, needed to believe magic was real. She was a girl who listened to stars, and she believed life was going to get better, that someday she would be free, safe, and protected. She needed hope like she needed air. Hope wasn't a luxury; it was a necessity.

Next, I needed to own hope, to possess it, to make it part of me. Standing in the shoes of my fortysomething self, it had seemed rational to justify being bitter, resentful, and unwilling to feel the vulnerability of childlike optimism. However, when I remembered myself as a little girl, it felt inhumane to take hope away from her. I was filled with compassion not only for the little child who had needed hope but also for the adult I'd become. That little girl was still a part of me, and she had believed in magic and goodness and singing stars. This part of me was worthy of love, attention, and care. I needed her as much as she'd needed hope.

So I held that image of me as a little girl in my mind. Even though it was difficult to open myself to the vulnerability of faith and trust, I was able to have compassion for the little me who had needed that sense of hope. By choosing compassion over bitterness, I slowly began to reclaim what I'd lost. It was a long process. I did not wake up one day, bright eyed and faithful. It was more tentative, less trusting, and hope was regained in inches, not miles. I couldn't just talk myself into being hopeful. It was more that I knew I'd rather live life with hope than without it. And then I started to make decisions and take action from a possibly hopeful place rather than reacting from a place of rationalized hopelessness.

But the work didn't stop there. Self-worth is built by reclaiming the lost self—by taking back the pieces that are rightfully yours, naming them, neutralizing them, and owning them. As you gain more of yourself, you experience a greater sense of what you're worth. However, to really live with an abiding sense of worthiness, you must practice living as your whole self. This means that you not only reclaim parts of yourself but that you take a specific action to celebrate and reinforce the importance of each part.

While I'd found compassion for the hopeful part of me, celebrating it would require me to do something special to honor this aspect. I wasn't sure how to celebrate hope. I thought about it for days and came up with nothing. Those days turned into weeks, and my sense of hope was still uncertain. It didn't exactly feel like something to celebrate. I was still careful and resistant to risk myself with the frivolity of hope. I was barely willing to dip a toe in. Celebrating hope would require a full nosedive, and I didn't feel ready.

It wasn't until one morning when I came down to the

kitchen to make coffee and I heard the tiny chirp of one lonely cricket that I realized what I needed to do. Standing there in the dark, I smiled and listened as it sang its little song. I didn't want it to stop, so I kept the lights off and started the kettle. It was a brisk autumn morning before sunrise. The sky was lavender, and I could see only a few stars. I sat at my kitchen table, listening to the song of that one tiny cricket, watching the stars as they and the cricket's song faded into the morning light. The act of listening to the night, being still in the darkness, would be my simple celebration of what I have come to call hope.

It's a small thing really, to be present and to listen to whatever the darkness brings, to open myself to the sounds of the night. This is how I celebrate the hope as who I am and who I was. This is how I celebrate what I've lost and what I've found. On summer nights, when the air is filled with the chorus of crickets, I listen to their music. This is my summer song of hope. I look up at the stars and remember who I was and where I came from. I listen to the song and I smile. In the winter, after the last of the crickets have finished the final trill of their late harvest songs, I listen still. I hear the wind, the rain, the ocean beating against the cliffs below my house. In that cold wildness, I hear my winter song of hope. And even in the darkest of those winter nights, I know the days will eventually get longer, and the evenings will get warmer, and once again, the sky will be filled with the chorus of crickets.

To reclaim hope, I didn't have to convince myself that life would get better. I didn't have to make promises of optimism that I couldn't keep. I didn't have to believe that wishes come true or that I have the power to influence them. I didn't have to stop being afraid of defeat, loss, and heart-ache. To reclaim hope, to find it within me, to own it and understand it and celebrate the childlike optimism of open-ended joy, I simply had to remember to listen to crickets and believe in the stars.

This is how I remember that even when things feel hope-less, I will be able to find my way back again and again. This is how I remind myself that every part—my hope and despair, my faith and distrust, my freedoms and failures, my light and my darkness—all of it belongs and all of it is necessary. This is how I remember that every part of me is worthy.

NAME IT

The first step in reclaiming the lost self is to give each aspect a specific name. Throughout the course of this book, you've learned several ways to become aware of aspects that have been lost. You can look to your unwritten rules. You can review defense mechanisms, the exiled villagers, and the ones who remained. You can look to what was lost in dysfunctional rela-tionship patterns where you may have fallen into emotional vampire or codependent tendencies. You might also simply find yourself triggered by something, similar to my experience in the hotel room or my bizarre reaction to being asked to pick up groceries. You might also find yourself bracing against pos-itive traits, like my example with hope.

> **Regardless of which particular aspect you're trying to reclaim, the work will be the same. You'll start by naming the quality, the feeling, the role, the adjective. You simply give that particular lost part a name.**

To be clear, at first many of these traits won't be something you necessarily want to own or reclaim. The work is to notice what has fallen into the shadow, to notice what your mind is defending against, to notice what you don't want to be called and what you don't want to feel. It's about noticing and naming what you don't allow yourself, what you resist, what you defend and justify. It's about naming the identities, experiences, feelings, desires, and needs that all belong to your complicated brilliance.

To build self-worth, you want to reclaim more of yourself—the good, the bad, the ugly, the beautiful. You want to own all of yourself—all your feelings, needs, desires. The more you allow yourself to name and reclaim, the greater your sense of self-worth. The mantra for this work is "You belong here. You are needed. Thank you." And this applies to every aspect. This work is about becoming whole. This means that all aspects belong, all are welcome, and every part of you is needed.

NEUTRALIZE IT

Before you can reclaim any aspect, you will need to neutralize it. This means you need to reduce the emotional charge, the judgment, the resistance, or the attachment to the aspect.

> **It's helpful to remember that you've never completely lost any part of yourself. You've only lost your awareness of it.**

All aspects are part of you, whether you want them to be or not. By repressing, denying, or shielding yourself from certain traits, you haven't eliminated them; you've only stopped recognizing your relationship to them.

You may feel an inner resistance, where you want to deflect or disown an aspect. You may find yourself wanting to shield yourself against a particular aspect. You might struggle with allowing yourself to be vulnerable or open to this step. This hesitancy is normal and to be expected because reclaiming aspects of yourself is uncomfortable and sometimes downright painful. To reclaim what you've lost, you must be willing to experience the discomfort associated with each aspect.

For example, to reclaim hope meant that I had to experience the discomfort associated with it. Namely, I had to be willing to risk the pain of disappointment, the pain of being betrayed, the pain of having my heart broken, and the pain of being further devastated. I'd lost hope in an unconscious attempt to avoid pain, but of course, that didn't work because there's no way to permanently avoid pain. By losing hope, I created the short-term relief of lowering my expectations, but I didn't escape the possibility of being let down; I merely caused myself to live in a permanent state of discouragement. I neutralized hope by recognizing that life would be painful with or without it. Losing hope hurt because it rendered life flat and meaningless. However, reclaiming hope would also hurt because it meant I had to be willing to risk disappointment, rejection, and heartbreak again. It was in recognizing the inevitability of pain that I was able to allow myself to soften. And in that softening, I realized that either way, I was going to be okay. Ironically, by surrendering and owning the possibility of pain, I began to connect to something hopeful within me.

By trying to avoid suffering, you will inevitably create more suffering. This is how it works with all aspects: where losing a piece of yourself may have created short-term relief, it always ends up creating long-term problems. By limiting your sense of self down to a smaller and smaller footprint instead of allowing yourself the generosity of a whole self, you live a life that's too small for you. And that always hurts.

Worthiness requires resilience. To live with an unwavering understanding of your own immeasurable value and to experience a steadfast understanding of your infinite worth, you must be able to endure and recover from challenges, setbacks, and adversity. It can be difficult and even painful to honor, respect, and care for every aspect of yourself. It is no small thing to look yourself in the eye without blinking. It takes courage to expose your flaws and your glory. It takes grit to own your losses and your victories. Worthiness requires all of you, and this means you must be strong enough to withstand a fair bit of suffering.

> **For every piece reclaimed, there will be pain to be acknowledged and reconciled.**

Sometimes that pain is grief, meaning you must mourn what was lost before you can embrace it again. Sometimes that pain is vulnerability, which requires an acute sense of putting yourself at risk and being willing to face the consequences of that risk.

Step-by-step, you move through each name and neutralize it. You welcome each part back home and reconcile both the pain of having lost access to it and the pain you must be willing to face by reclaiming it. Eventually, you feel a shift where there's no longer resistance to the idea. It may be a subtle shift where a particular aspect has lost its charge. And sometimes it's a radical shift, where there's a significant change in your experience. Sometimes it happens in a moment, and sometimes the process can take months.

> # The mind is incredible, and it knows how to heal itself.

To regain access to the lost parts of you, you must determine that they are necessary and that the loss has not ultimately prevented suffering. Go slowly and gently through this process, and try not to hurry through it. Your mind won't let go of the resistance until it is ready. When it's ready, letting go of the old pain and welcoming yourself back home becomes effortless. Trust the memories that surface, and follow the bread crumbs to where they take you. Do what you can to open your mind and heart, to drop resistance and have compassion for who you were and who you are. Welcome every part of you. No part is unworthy. Everything belongs. Every part is needed.

OWN IT

A worthy mind doesn't need to disown any part of itself. It doesn't need to argue against itself. It is open to experiencing the entirety of your emotions. It welcomes your needs. It allows what you love. It honors your deepest desires. To reclaim your lost self, you must not only be willing to break the unwritten rules, you must be willing to abolish them. This means you not only neutralize every aspect, you are willing to own any and every answer to these questions:

- *Who am I?*
- *What do I feel?*
- *What do I need?*
- *What do I love?*
- *What do I really want?*

> *Who am I?* **A worthy mind is willing to own all identities. It is open to all adjectives, roles, and characteristics.**

This requires that you do not see certain aspects as good and others as bad. The mantra for this is "I'm allowed to be this." If you have a particularly difficult time owning that aspect, you can use the mantra "I'm allowed to be this sometimes." In a worthy mind, you are allowed to be introverted. You are allowed to be too much. You're allowed to be stupid sometimes. You're allowed to be smart sometimes as well. The work is to rewrite your identity rules so that you give yourself permission to own every trait at least some of the time or under certain circumstances. The goal isn't to attach to a label; it is to become more like Teflon, where nothing sticks. For example, instead of trying to prove that you aren't selfish, the work is to give that characteristic permission to be part of your makeup: "I am allowed to be selfish sometimes."

The goal is to allow any aspect to be part of you without feeling like you need to defend or deflect. A worthy mind doesn't attach itself to positive labels and ignore the negative labels. A worthy mind allows itself to own a trait and then lets it go.

> **What do I feel? A worthy mind is willing to feel all of it. It is open to the vast expansiveness of your emotional and physical body.**

This requires that you do not see certain emotions or physical experiences as good and others as bad. Every inner experience belongs, they are all needed, and they are all welcome. The mantra for this is "I'm allowed to feel this." A worthy mind allows you to be sensitive, sad, upset, and angry. In a worthy mind, you're allowed to be hot, cold, hungry, and full. In a worthy mind, you're allowed to be hopeful, proud, and full of joy. The goal is to be able to be open to your inner experience so that you can respond to the emotional and physical feedback being offered. Instead of trying to subdue certain emotions or avoid particular sensations, you begin to see them as neutral feedback that is welcome, helpful, and necessary.

What do I need? **A worthy mind is willing to need what it needs. It is deeply attentive to your individual needs.**

This requires you to be neutral about your desires for security, self-preservation, and what it takes for you to feel nurtured and protected. Every need is valid, and every need wants to be acknowledged. The mantra for this is "I'm allowed to need this." For example, you are allowed to need human touch. You are allowed to need a hug. You are allowed to need attention. You are allowed to need your mom, a friend, someone to love. A worthy mind welcomes and appreciates your individual needs. It does not see what you need as something to be ashamed of or something to hide. It wants you to feel secure, safe, and held. A worthy mind is open to your neediness and is willing to listen and respond to those needs.

What do I love? **A worthy mind is willing to love what it loves. It is open to every experience of attachment,**

> connection, and love. It celebrates what you care about, who you care about, and why you care.

This requires that you do not see some types of love as good and others as bad. It means that everything, everyone, and every reason that you experience love and connection are valid and welcome. The mantra for this is "I'm allowed to love." In a worthy mind, you're allowed to love whatever you want. You're allowed to love chocolate, punk rock, and hairless cats. In a worthy mind, love is never wrong. It is welcomed, allowed, and celebrated.

> *What do I really want?* A worthy mind is willing to want what it wants. It will acknowledge every desire, no matter how seemingly frivolous.

This requires that you do not see some desires as good and others as bad. It means that what you want deserves your attention and respect. The mantra for this is "I am allowed to want this." If that mantra is too difficult to believe, you can add the word "sometimes." For example, you are allowed to want fancy clothes, you are allowed to want a hot sex life, and you are allowed to want a best friend. You are allowed to want anything you want. The goal here isn't necessarily to make these wants come true but merely to open a neutral channel where you have access to your desires without censoring them or silencing them. In a worthy mind, every desire is valid, and all are welcome.

CELEBRATE IT

Once you've honored what's been lost and done the emotional and cognitive work to welcome a part of you, the final step in reclaiming your lost self is to celebrate what you've regained. "Celebrate" means doing something special or meaningful to honor the event. So the final step is to do something special or meaningful to honor each aspect. And this is the most important part. Merely thinking about reclaiming yourself doesn't work. You want to reinforce the idea that this part of you holds intrinsic value, that it deserves your care and respect, that it is worthy. You want to take a deliberate action that reinforces the idea that this part deserves your time, attention, and energy. You want to take an action that invites that aspect to come alive again. This means you practice embodying this aspect by associating it with an action, thought, ritual, or behavior.

> **Worthiness wants you to celebrate all of you. The good parts, the bad parts, the shameful parts, the strong parts. This means bringing forward, acknowledging, and taking an intentional action to honor each part of you.**

There is no right or wrong way to celebrate. The goal is to find an action that will be personal and individual to your history. The objective isn't to merely see your work as a mental exercise but to take action to bring your work into real life. You're looking for an action that reinforces worthiness. You're looking to do something that reinforces the idea that this aspect of you deserves your time, energy, and attention.

Maybe you celebrate your desire for coziness by wearing your favorite sweater. Each time you wrap yourself up in the fuzzy warmth, you remind yourself that you are worth honoring your desires. By wearing the sweater, you reinforce the idea that your desires are not only welcome but worth celebrating.

Maybe you celebrate reclaiming your boundaries by opting out of a texting thread that you no longer want to be involved in. By acknowledging this, following through, and taking action, you practice setting boundaries and celebrate that boundary.

Celebration doesn't have to be a large thing; in fact, sometimes the most powerful celebrations are actions that simply confirm your feelings, desires, and needs.

In my example of reclaiming hunger, my celebration was the meal planning and food prepping and providing burgers for my friends at the cabin. To honor the part of me who was hungry and to intentionally celebrate this part of me, I made individual meals for myself for the entire weekend. Breakfast, lunch, and dinner were premade and stored in my ice cooler. This was something special, a way that I could commemorate and show respect for a part of me who had been silenced. This reinforced that my hunger was worthy of my own time, attention, and energy. It was something that I could honor and protect. It was something that mattered. It was a way to demonstrate radical kindness for myself. This was how I honored my younger self who had been so hungry and my older self who had been so triggered.

In my postdivorce example, when I didn't know what flowers I liked, what movie to watch, or if I liked bell peppers, the celebration was the act of giving these things to myself. To give myself the opportunity to taste a bell pepper and then decide. To put yellow flowers on my kitchen table for the simple reason that they made me smile. To rent 27 Dresses and give myself permission to watch all the chick flicks I wanted. These small wins, these tiny celebrations all reinforced that I was worth knowing. By intentionally choosing to honor these tiny wins, I became more familiar with who I was, what I felt, and what I loved.

Regardless of who you are and what aspect you are

reclaiming, your celebration should honor the aspect, respect what was lost, revere what has been found, and reinforce a sense of worthiness. It can be something private and quiet, like the act of listening for crickets. It can be something more public, like throwing yourself a party. It can be something brave, like publishing your poetry for the very first time. It can be something rebellious, like voting against the political party you were raised to support. It can be something joyful, like dancing in the mirror in your underwear. Or it can be solemn, like burning a letter to honor your grief. No matter how you choose to celebrate, the intention is to welcome all parts of yourself back home and take meaningful action to reinforce the idea that every single part of you is worthy.

BECOMING WHOLE

As you reclaim and celebrate each lost aspect of yourself, you occupy more and more of your whole self. You bring light and awareness to every part of you. You drop your resistance and open yourself to every possibility with you. This means that every time you come up against an inner argument, something that you don't want to be, don't want to feel, don't want to need, love, or want, you drop the struggle and instead give yourself permission to name it, neutralize it, own it, and celebrate it. The greater the resistance, the more you may need to soften the permission. The goal isn't to own only ultrapositive ideas, nor is it to own only terribly negative ideas. The goal is to see both as necessary, both as part of you, and both as part of being a whole human being.

Sometimes this will look like rewriting an old story and accepting something that you learned to deny. Sometimes this will look like noticing where you're triggered and doing some sleuth work to figure out what might be hiding in the shadow. The work is to neutralize any internal defense against a particular characteristic and then to welcome and celebrate the characteristic. You can look to your unwritten rules and rewrite them. You can bring awareness to your unconscious defense mechanisms and actively change them. You can change dysfunctional relationships by empowering yourself with boundaries. You can notice who you internally criticize and then do the work to own the aspects within yourself.

This process unveils the unwavering knowledge of your intrinsic worth. Rather than constantly trying to cut off the pieces that aren't acceptable or trying to shape-shift into what others want, by owning your whole self, you are willing to take up space, use your voice, and advocate for your needs. By no longer playing small, you become unstoppable.

> **This process isn't about trying to be better; it's about dropping all resistance to who you are, who you have been, and who you are becoming.**

It's about being willing to say yes to all of it. It's about being willing to own the good, the bad, the selfish, the stupid, the brilliant, the strong, and the weak. It's about noticing the struggle within you, softening into the shadow, and allowing yourself permission to have flaws, to have needs, to make mistakes, and to be forgiven.

This process takes time, and it deserves your attention, your energy, and your respect. Each aspect matters. As you gain pieces of yourself, you will find that you gain an inner momentum. At first, this work may feel like a struggle. You may not want to own pieces that you've conditioned yourself to hate, resist, or plainly deny. You may not want to forgive yourself or neutralize an aspect. You may be afraid of letting yourself off the hook. That is all normal, and that is exactly how the lost self keeps itself hidden. However, as you do this work, you will find that for every aspect you allow, you gain a sense of lightness, and for every piece that you neutralize and celebrate, you gain self-worth. Eventually, you'll get to a point where your worthy mind is willing to own anything and celebrating everything.

First, name it. Choose an entity, characteristic, or part of you that you want to reclaim, and give the aspect a specific name.

Ask yourself: *What is the name of this identity, feeling, need, love, or desire?*

Second, neutralize it. If it's a particularly difficult idea to work with, imagine yourself as a small child as you do this work. Neutralize the pain attached to this aspect by articulating the discomfort or suffering that was caused by losing access to this aspect, and determine what discomfort will be required to reclaim the aspect.

Ask yourself: *Losing this part of me hurt because [fill in the blank]. Reclaiming this part of me will hurt because [fill in the blank].*

Third, own it. Next, give yourself permission to own and accept this part of you. If it's particularly difficult to own, you can use the word "sometimes" to soften any inner resistance.

Tell yourself: *I'm allowed to own this part of me.* If you feel resistance to this idea, tell yourself: *I'm allowed to own this part of me sometimes.*

Fourth, celebrate it. Celebrate this aspect by doing something special or enjoyable to honor it. This means you take deliberate and intentional action to reinforce the idea that this aspect is worth your time, energy, and attention.

Ask yourself: *What action can I take to reinforce the idea that this aspect deserves time, attention, and respect?*

It's important to note that sometimes this four-step process can happen within the span of a few minutes. Other times, it may take months to fully name, neutralize, own, and reclaim what was lost. There is no right or wrong way to do this work, so please trust yourself as you move through it. If it feels too difficult to work with a particular aspect, just skip it and move on to the next one. The intention of this work is to remove the inner struggle, not to create more burden for yourself. The more you do this work, the easier it becomes.

Real Stories: Melinda

Melinda wanted to gain the courage to date again. She worked from home, most of her free time was devoted to work, and she tended to keep to a small circle of friends. She had been badly hurt in her previous relationship and was still recovering from a brutal breakup. She had tried dating but tended to be drawn to unavailable men who kept her at arm's length. She continually tried to be at peace with being single and told herself that she needed to be optimistic and strong. But secretly, when she was really honest with herself, she realized that she was painfully lonely and really wanted intimacy and connection. Her life had become small, consisting mostly of her work and few outings. She shared, "I realized that the more I try to tell myself that I should be happy being alone, the more I deny an important part of myself. Ugh, this part makes me cringe. I just hate it. But what I'm learning is that this is the part of me that I need to reclaim and own, and I'm committed to doing this work. So here it is: This part of me is named Needy. It's the part of me that I am most ashamed of and the part of me that I most try to hide and erase."

Melinda said she had a difficult time trying to neutralize the pain around accepting this neediness in her. She had lived most of her life trying to cover this up, trying to deny it, or completely ignoring this part of herself. She explained that this quality of neediness was something toxic and sticky and something that she had always abhorred. Her unwritten rules from childhood centered around being strong, capable, intelligent, and self-reliant. Neediness was the antithesis to this, and she had a lot of resistance to owning it. However, her last breakup had broken her in a way that she hadn't been able to repair or recover from, and this was painfully affecting her dating life. She said, "I feel raw and unprotected. I can't fake my way into that strong, capable facade any longer. The real me, the one behind the mask, she has been hurt, she is wounded, and she is vulnerable. But that feels so fantastically dangerous to admit to myself, let alone to another human being. I find neediness so distasteful, and I'd be gutted if someone saw me in that way. Maybe that's why I tend to go for the unavailable guy. It keeps me from having to show up."

Melinda had spent most of her life making a case against neediness. She saw it as a liability, a hardship, a burden to bear. This is why it's so important to look at both sides of the pain. Sharing, expressing, and admitting needs or neediness requires an intense amount of vulnerability and inner strength. Vulnerability puts you at tremendous risk for pain. Sharing your needs opens the possibility to being ridiculed, being rejected, or even worse: being ignored. On the flip side, however, there is also pain. By denying, dismissing, or disregarding the needy part of you, you must endure a different type of pain: an insatiable inner restlessness that is never cared for and is never acknowledged. This underlying discomfort hums under everything that you do and erodes any foundation of self-worth.

I explained this to her and had her fill in the blanks for the next part of the exercise. She took a few moments, and then something seemed to click. She said, "Oh, I get it. Losing neediness hurts because now I feel lonely and disconnected. And reclaiming neediness will hurt because I might be rejected again. Both ways hurt."

I agreed. "Yes, but now you get to choose which pain you want. Do you want the pain of denying your needs? Or do you want the pain of possibly being rejected for honoring your needs?"

"Well, when you put it that way, I'd rather take a chance on being rejected by someone else. But that also means I would stop being rejected by my own self. I can handle that. I'm glad we looked at the high side and low side for this because it was equally freeing to see that the 'good' qualities aren't objectively and irrefutably and always good. They have a cost too, especially if they're held on to too tightly or made part of identity. Trying to always be strong or self-reliant hasn't exactly fixed the part of me that is wounded and raw."

"Do you think you are ready to own this? Could you say that you are needy and feel neutral about it?" I asked.

Melinda thought a moment before she said, "I really want to say yes. But there's still a lot of resistance in me. I want to be someone who's cool with it, but I'm just not."

Reclaiming something that you've spent most of your life resisting is going to take some patience and a lot of practice. However, by softening the idea, you can start to take baby steps toward reclaiming it. You can do this by making a case for why you want to drop your resistance to the characteristic. Simply list reasons for why it would be helpful or important to drop the resistance. In Melinda's case, it could be helpful to drop resistance to neediness so that she could learn to honor her needs in real time. It could be important to drop resistance to neediness so that she could see when someone else wasn't honoring her needs. It could be important to drop her resistance to neediness because she might meet someone who wants to be able to share that part of themselves without being judged or shamed. The work here is to continue giving your mind reasons to drop the argument and to relax into allowing every part to have a voice.

I shared this with Melinda. She nodded slowly as she listened, taking it all in.

"So could you say that you are needy sometimes? Or that it's okay to be needy sometimes? Or could you even soften it further by saying it's okay for some people to be needy sometimes?"

Melinda thought about it and said, "It's so interesting to observe myself through this process. It's like I'm at war with myself, and I don't want to let this part of me in. I fight and argue and my whole body is tight. But then as you were talking, I noticed that I started to relax, and for some reason, it doesn't seem so bad anymore. Maybe it's because we've said the word 'needy' so many times that it's lost its power?"

"Or maybe it's just lost its emotional charge," I said. "So let's keep going. The next step is to give yourself permission to own this part. It's really about giving yourself another reason to drop the resistance, allow this work to unfold, and open yourself to becoming whole."

"Yes, actually that feels pretty easy now," Melinda said.

"I'm allowed to own the needy part of me. I have permission to own that part of me. Definitely."

This work isn't a one-and-done type of work. For Melinda to make lasting changes and ultimately reclaim access to this part of her, she would need to take this practice into her real life. Every time she found herself wanting to hide her needs, her practice would be to drop in and remind herself that it was okay to be needy. Whenever she found herself harshly judging neediness in herself or in others, her mantra would be "It is okay to be needy sometimes."

As she brought this practice into her everyday life, she determined that a way to celebrate her neediness would be to wrap herself in a blanket. As she traced her history for clues as to how to celebrate her neediness, she kept coming back to the same memory of being told that she was too old to have a "blankie." She said that her blankie was way that she self-soothed as a child. She shared, "To be honest, I felt that giving myself a blankie sounded kind of dumb and frivolous. But I pushed through that and did the exercise anyway. I found this old blanket in my linen closet. I've had it since college, and I never use it because it doesn't match my aesthetic. But last night, I felt that terrible sense of longing, loneliness, desperation. I went and got that old ugly blanket and wrapped it around myself, and I told myself it was okay to be needy. I couldn't believe the power in offering myself this small kindness. I sat on the floor and leaned against the closet door, and I just sobbed. It was like something in me finally felt seen."

Real Stories: Hanna

Hanna wanted help determining her career path. She had just
completed a degree in accounting and had several job offers,
yet she felt uninspired and reluctant to accept any of them.
She was afraid that she had invested her time and money on a
degree that didn't interest her any longer, yet she was unsure
what to do about it. She had chosen her degree to prevent
her from repeating her parents' mistakes. As a child, she had
been acutely aware of her parents' financial difficulties, and
she resented their lifestyle. Her parents had pieced together
odd jobs, sold handmade knickknacks at craft fairs, and never
knew where the next paycheck was coming from. She shared,
"I chose this career path because I never wanted to be irresponsible like my parents. But here I am with a few job offers, and
I'm paralyzed with dread. I realized that I just wanted to be an
accountant to prove that I'm not like my parents. But that's no
way to live my life. I think I need to reclaim something here,
but I keep coming up against resistance and can't quite figure it
out. I think it has something to do with my career, but it's like
my mind won't even let me think it."

She said she couldn't quite name the aspect that she
needed to reclaim, so she spent time retracing her history. She
tried to remember things that she had loved as a child and as a
teenager. She tried to remember her favorite classes, her favorite topics. She said one particular memory kept surfacing, and
she thought maybe it was related to this work. She shared that
she had received a scholarship to participate in a summer art
program.

She said, "My parents didn't have money for extras like art camp, and I remember how proud they were that I'd received a scholarship. They were prouder of that than anything I'd ever achieved at school. I remember them saying that I was an artist, that I was just like them. And I hated that. I didn't want to be just like them. But that's not the memory that keeps coming back. What I keep remembering was the ceramic room at that camp. I remember what it felt like, what it smelled like. I remember my hands in the clay. I remember being sad when the day was done and I had to go home. I wanted to stay in that place forever."

Even though Hanna couldn't quite see the aspect she had lost, her childhood memories seemed to give an indication as to what needed to be reclaimed. In our sessions, I had noticed that when she spoke about accounting and about her job prospects, there was an edge of resentment in her voice. She had shared that her career path had deliberately been chosen because of her judgments about her parents. Yet when she spoke about art camp and the ceramic room in particular, she spoke with reverence, kindness, and gratitude. My hunch was that she had denied something she loved because she linked it to the pain of her parents' financial problems. This is a common kind of splitting, where someone reduces a complicated matter to a simplified idea. However, financial problems cannot be reduced to the simple idea of having nontraditional employment. There are people with great paying jobs that end up with devastating financial problems. And there are people with sporadic and unreliable income sources that end up financially stable.

I explained this to Hanna and said, "You mentioned that when you received the art camp scholarship, your parents said you were an artist, just like them. What do you think of the term 'artist'? Is that something that you resonate with for yourself? Do you have any judgments about that word?"

"Do I have any judgments about the word? How much time do you have?" Hanna laughed. "To me, the word 'artist' is the same as being irresponsible, broke, and totally selfish."

"But what about in the ceramic room? If you can just drop your story about your parents and simply allow the little you to stand in the ceramic room, I think that part of you loved art," I said.

"She did love art. I did. I think I still do," Hanna said.

"Can you imagine what it would be like if you allowed yourself to reclaim the title of artist? Can you imagine what it would be like if there was no static, no resentment, no disappointment attached to that quality?"

"I think it would be amazing. It sounds like freedom."

To be able to reclaim the identity of artist, she'd need to neutralize and reconcile the pain attached to having lost that aspect and to regaining the aspect. She had lost her inner artist because she related it to financial irresponsibility and selfishness. By trying to avoid being financially irresponsible and selfish, she followed a career path that was uninspiring for her. She followed money and lost something that she dearly loved. Yet to reclaim her inner artist, there would be a different type of pain to bear. She would need to believe in herself, she'd need to trust her heart, and she'd need to be willing to be uncertain.

I explained this to her and asked, "Can you fill in the blank? Losing the artist in me hurt because..."

Hanna thought for a moment. "Because I lost something I loved. It feels so sad to admit that."

"And reclaiming the artist will hurt because..."

"Well, it's not exactly hurt, but it's uncomfortable. Reclaiming the artist in me will be uncomfortable because it's unfamiliar, uncharted, a little scary."

"Why are you allowed to own the artist in you? Why should you own the artist in you?" I asked.

"I think I need to own this because it's a huge blind spot in my soul. It's like I've spent the past six years trying to avoid this part of me and trying to talk myself into being something that I'm not. But then when I had to actually accept a job, I felt paralyzed. I didn't know what to do. I felt lost."

Hanna had come to the coursework for guidance on her career decisions, and it could be tempting for her to want to attach a career path to a newly reclaimed identity. However, this work isn't about a career path; it is about becoming whole. It's about widening the scope of who you believe you are. It's about saying yes to all aspects and seeing that they all belong.

Hanna had a part of her that was an accountant. She also had a part of her that was an artist. She probably also had a thousand other parts of her that might lead to lucrative, fulfilling, and meaningful careers. All identities belong, and all deserve respect and kindness. I urged her to try to keep her career questions separate and to simply do the work to open herself up to all possibilities. She had lived most of her life and chosen her college path based on limiting herself to a narrow idea of not becoming her parents. By reclaiming every aspect of herself and by being willing to celebrate these aspects, she would see that there were hundreds of paths to choose from and that all of them had positives and negatives. By doing this work, she'd strengthen her connection to who she is, what she feels, and what she needs, loves, and wants. She would be able to tap into this inner guidance as she navigated her career questions. Without access to her whole self, she was paralyzed, uninspired, and lost. By welcoming and reclaiming her whole self, she had an inner compass that she could rely on.

I challenged her to celebrate the artist identity in a way that had nothing to do with a career path. She chose to celebrate by signing up for lessons at a local ceramics studio. She shared, "I thought about going back to school to study art or to take a ceramics class, but that felt like I'd fall into the trap of trying to make art into a profession. So instead, I found a little studio that's run by a quirky lady here in town, and I signed up for lessons with her. It's the opposite of a résumé item; it's something that is simply for me. I still don't know what I'm going to be when I grow up, but I do know that when I am sitting at the wheel, hands covered in clay, it feels like I've come home to myself."

Real Stories: Kara

Kara wanted to strengthen her sense of self-worth. She had left her career in corporate America the previous year to pursue her dream of opening a yoga studio. However, she found that entrepreneurship was much more difficult than she had imagined. She struggled with managing staff and teachers and was a self-proclaimed doormat. If a teacher asked for the day off, she would automatically pick up the slack. If a student asked for a discount, she felt that she had to no choice but to mark down her prices. She shared, "For most of my life, I have felt subpar. I was never great in school. I was mediocre in corporate America. I had hoped that by following my dreams, I'd finally be different. This work has shown me how much I identify with the word 'dud,' and I'm so sick of it. This goes back all the way to childhood. My sister was a standout star, and I was the dud, always in her shadow."

She said that she was quite comfortable with the negative labels and very resistant to owning anything positive about herself. She admitted that even in her business, she downplayed her abilities. She said she had more training and more qualifications than any other teacher at the studio, but she didn't list them in her bio because she didn't want to outshine anyone. She said, "Maybe I need to reclaim the idea of dud? There's definitely something here that I resist. I definitely don't want to be a show-off, and I don't want to be an attention grabber. I'd rather just stay on the sidelines. I'm not sure what I'm supposed to reclaim."

Kara's confusion was understandable. When working with the lost self, you are by definition working with something that you have difficulty accepting or recognizing, and this can be perplexing. A rule of thumb to keep in mind is that the aspect that you most resist will likely be the part that you most need to reclaim. If you're stuck, try to figure out the aspect that you don't want to be or try not to be seen as; this is a good indication that you've lost access to that very thing. A worthy mind welcomes all parts, so resistance to any particular aspect shows what still needs to be recovered.

In Kara's case, she was not only aware of the dud identity, she was pretty comfortable with it. However, she was quite resistant to the flip side. Although her humility may have been well intentioned, playing small had been a detriment to her self-worth and was negatively affecting her business. Kara's conscious insistence that she was a dud and that she didn't want to be a show-off pointed to an unconscious inability to see herself as a winner or to acknowledge the part of her that might want some attention.

I explained this to her and said, "I don't think you need to reclaim the part of you that feels like a dud. I think you need to reclaim part of you that believes the exact opposite. If you think about this entity called Dud, what would you name the opposite entity? Imagine this part of you that is willing to be in the spotlight, the part of you that wants attention, the part of you that might want to show off a little."

Kara covered her face with her hands as if hiding from the question. She groaned and then answered, "I really don't want to say because I know you're going to make me own it."

"Probably," I said with a smile.

"It's what we used to call my sister, Superstar. It definitely didn't mean anything good. In my family, it meant someone who needed attention, who wanted praise, or who needed to be in the limelight. I think of all the times that my sister made the entire family sit down and watch one of her plays that she wrote. We'd sit rolling our eyes and laughing at her behind her back. It was a grind. We called her the little superstar. She always thought it was a compliment. It wasn't."

Kara's history with this word made an even bigger case for reclaiming it. My heart hurt for Kara's sister, as I imagined a little girl asking her family to watch her, wanting an audience, not realizing that she was opening herself to her family's covert ridicule. I could see how little Kara learned that it was safer to be on the sidelines. Kara lost access to this part of herself because in her experience, being a superstar was equivalent to humiliation.

Reclaiming the lost self is about neutralizing all aspects so that you don't see one as all good and the other as all bad. A worthy mind isn't reductive; it's flexible and open. In Kara's case, she'd need to learn that the title of Dud may have helped her avoid the pain of humiliation, yet it created the chronic suffering of debilitating insecurity. On the flip side, denying her inner superstar may have given her the illusion of safety, but ultimately it prevented her from achieving what she deserved. The goal would be to see the idea of dud as sometimes good and sometimes bad and to also see the idea of superstar as sometimes good and sometimes bad.

I explained this to her and said, "With as much compassion as you can possibly muster, imagine yourself as an adult, sitting next to little you while you watched your sister's superstar show. Imagine celebrating her courage rather than joining in with disparaging her. Imagine applauding your sister's performance. Maybe go even further and give her a standing ovation. What would that feel like?"

Whispering, Kara said, "It feels true, like of course I'd want to celebrate her courage. It's heartbreaking to think about it. To realize how brave she was and how cruel we were."

"So take all that compassion and empathy and offer that to the part of you who wants to be a superstar too. This part of you is courageous. This part of you wants to be seen and heard. This part of you wants recognition, attention, maybe even a standing ovation. Embody that deep well of compassion, and offer it to yourself. What would happen if you could drop your resistance so that you could access your inner superstar?"

"I could see that it might be helpful to be able to call on this part of me when I'm teaching or when I need to be more of a leader," Kara said.

"That's a great first step. So now, let's fill in the blank. 'Losing your inner superstar hurt because...'" I said.

Kara thought for a moment and then said, "Because it kept me afraid of success. It kept me small and apologetic. It made me into a dud."

"And reclaiming your inner superstar will hurt because..."

"Because I might be ridiculed and humiliated. I won't be able to hide anymore. I will need to be brave, and that's definitely outside my comfort zone."

Kara's work going forward would be to continue to embody her inner superstar. This wasn't easy for her, but she learned to embrace this side of her in little ways. She started by being more outspoken at work, and she'd make a joke about her inner superstar wanting attention. At the end of staff meetings, she'd kid about wanting applause. Over time, she seemed to be more comfortable with her superstar self, and rather than using self-deprecating humor, she had more self-compassion and kindness. Weeks later, she shared, "It's taken me a long time to be comfortable in the spotlight. And although I was so resistant to owning my inner superstar, I can say that it has been completely life changing. Last week, I signed up for an acting class. I don't even recognize myself. I saw an ad for the class, and something in me lit up. Like, I want to do that! It felt old, deep, soul-level real. I snatched the flyer and stuck it in my purse and signed up the minute I got home. I can't think of a better way to celebrate my inner superstar."

YOUR WORTHY WORK:
Reclaiming Your Lost Self

Now it's your turn. Choose an entity, characteristic, or part of you that you want to reclaim, and give the aspect a specific name.

First, name it. Trace your history, sift through your memories, and do what you can to try to name the specific quality, characteristic, feeling, or desire that you may have lost.

Ask yourself: *What is the name of this identity, feeling, need, love, or desire?*

Second, neutralize it. If it's a particularly difficult idea to work with, imagine yourself as a small child as you do this work. Neutralize the pain attached to this aspect by articulating the discomfort or suffering that was caused by losing access to this aspect, and determine what discomfort will be required to reclaim the aspect.

Ask yourself: *Losing this part of me hurt because [fill in the blank]. Reclaiming this part of me will hurt because [fill in the blank].*

Third, own it. Next, give yourself permission to own and accept this part of you. If it's particularly difficult to own, you can use the word "sometimes" to soften any inner resistance. The goal is to be willing to own all of yourself, to give yourself permission to be, feel, need, love, and want anything and everything.

Tell yourself: *I'm allowed to own this part of me.* If you feel resistance to this idea, tell yourself: *I'm allowed to own this part of me sometimes.*

Fourth, celebrate it. Celebrate that aspect by doing something special or enjoyable to honor the aspect. This means you take deliberate and intentional action to reinforce the idea that this aspect is worth your time, energy, and attention.

Ask yourself: *What action can I take to reinforce the idea that this aspect deserves time, attention, and respect?*

Please remember that sometimes this four-step process can happen within the span of a few minutes. Other times, it may take months to fully name, neutralize, own, and reclaim what was lost. There is no right or wrong way to do this work, so please trust yourself as you move through it. If it feels too difficult to work with a particular aspect, just skip it and move on to the next one. The intention of this work is to remove the inner struggle, not to create more burden for yourself. The more you do this work, the easier it becomes.

JOURNAL PROMPTS

1. When you consider reclaiming aspects of yourself, do you find it easier to own positive or negative traits? Why might one idea be more difficult than another?

2. What is your relationship to the word "celebrate"? What memories or experiences come to mind when you think about the idea of celebration?

3. What part of this work do you most resist? Why might there be an inner resistance to that particular part of the work?

Epilogue

Over the past few years, life has changed radically for most of us. Through lockdowns, isolation, and illness, we have not only lost each other, our families and loved ones, our jobs, and our hoped-for futures, but many of us have also lost ourselves. We've lost who we had known ourselves to be. Of course, we've gained things as well. We have found joys in small moments. We have found new ways to connect. We have taken up knitting, bread baking, and gardening. We have adopted pets, read stacks of books, and belly laughed at goofy TikToks.

There have been times in my life when I haven't really noticed what had been lost. Times when I slowly lost myself in tiny invisible ways and then ended up at a crossroads where I no longer knew who I was. There have been other times in my life when I seemed to have landed in a stranger's life overnight, where it appears as if everything I knew about myself suddenly and uncomfortably had fallen away. This is where I recently found myself, with an unfamiliar empty nest, a daughter at college, living an hour away from the nearest town, and newly married.

For nearly twenty years, I knew who I was. I was a mother, a provider, a protector. I woke up, made lunches, organized backpacks, made sure beds were made and teeth were brushed. I made money, bought groceries, and paid the rent. I locked the doors, closed the curtains, and double-checked the side door before I went to sleep. My life had a rhythm and a purpose. I knew what I had to do. I knew who I had to be.

I think it was always going to be hard to be on this side of motherhood. I knew I might feel adrift or a little lost once she left home. But I had no idea how much grief I would feel, how lost I would feel, or how meaningless life would feel without the gravity of daily motherhood holding me onto the surface of this planet.

Beyond the abrupt change in mothering duties, I was also trying to find my legs in country living. The days had a different pace. There was no running off to the store if I forgot something. There was no downtown where I could spend an afternoon window shopping. There was beauty and grandeur. There were mountains and oceans and sky. It is a good life, yet it is a markedly quiet life. And to be frank, I wasn't quite sure what to do with myself yet.

This unknown landscape, this lack of direction, this beautiful, open, and generous life I had in front of me scared me.

The uncharted nature, the open horizons, the lack of minute-to-minute scheduling was dauntingly empty.

Often, reclaiming your lost self is about repurposing aspects that seem dark, unwanted, or even shameful. These are the failures, the broken parts, the deplorable parts that you must not only forgive but learn to love. These are things that you had once deemed shameful, harmful, or unworthy. You collect your emotions, your flaws, your wounds, and you turn them into something beautiful, meaningful, necessary. That part of the process is about giving shelter and support to the wild little you who felt that the only way to survive was to surrender these things to the shadows. It's about rewriting a story that was once ugly and hidden and turning it into one of beauty and meaning.

However, there are other times when this work is more about redemption. It's about regaining possession of something that you unintentionally surrendered. It's the process of taking back those cherished aspects that were never meant to be pawned, brokered, or given away. It's about reconnecting with who you used to be, what you used to feel, and what you used to love. It's about coming home.

Through death, divorce, and plenty of failures, I have stood in places where I was completely unknown to myself, times when I needed to rewrite old stories and reclaim the forgotten pieces of my past. But here, in midlife, I find myself needing to trace my story back further. I need to go back to a time when I could remember what I'd loved, how I had felt, what I had desired. Who I was before motherhood, career, the daily responsibilities.

I do not want to just sleepwalk through life and become less and less of myself. I have fought too hard and too long to silently surrender myself. I want to reclaim all of myself, to own my past, my wounds, my scars. I want to forgive my mistakes and shortcomings. I want to stretch my arms and legs in all directions, to take up all the space available to me. I want to own my laughter and my heartache. I want to feel free within myself without trying to hide or shelter any part of me. I want to own the brightest and the blackest parts of myself. I want to sing, lie in the summer grass, and inhale all of life.

When I think about reclaiming what's been unintentionally abandoned, I think of the optimism and hope that I'd once had for my future. I think of endless possibilities and opportunities. I think of the feeling of youth, the sense of having so much life out in front of me. I think of wanderlust and a sense of adventure. Before I was a mother, a wife, a teacher, an author, there was certainly a me. She was interesting, alive, driven, and fun, and I want to know her again. She is the me at the center of my life. The me who I have known by heart. The me I forgot and had to rediscover again and again.

So I walk and trace my steps back to places I've known. I ask myself, *Who did I used to be?* I was a student, a piano teacher. I was a woman, a mountain biker. I was a roommate, an artist. I was pretty and smart. All these still belong to me. All these deserve attention, recognition, and celebration.

I ask myself, *What did I used to feel?* I close my eyes and try to remember. I remember feeling capable and strong. Most of all, I remember feeling alive, a feeling of vitality coursing through me. And even though it seems so far away now, a bygone era, I want to believe that I can have this again, that I can own it, celebrate it, not like I did in my twenties, but the type of vitality that can only come with maturity.

I ask myself, *What did I used to need?* I remember needing human touch, the grandeur of nature, and time alone. I remember needing safety and security. I needed a sense of meaning and purpose. These needs are still valid and still alive in me.

I ask myself, *What did I used to love?* I remember loving my piano so fiercely. I remember dancing in ballrooms and clubs and barns and fairgrounds. I remember the lessons, the teachers. I remember smiling. All those memories are still in these bones.

I ask myself, *What did I really want?* I remember wanting a place to call home, a family that felt safe. I wanted to belong to someone. I wanted to love and be loved. And even though I have these things now, it is important to remember to want what I have. It's important to celebrate what I wanted and honor what those desires created. And to not forget the road that brought me here.

This morning, I picked up a magazine and thumbed through it while I drank my cup of coffee. There were pictures of skiers, rock climbers, mountain bikers, the snow. There was an advertisement for an annual cross-country ski race, one that I used to look forward to every year. I'd completely forgotten about it, and something lit up within me, a feeling of familiarity, like seeing a long-lost friend. And then I realized that flipping through the pictures, I was remembering me from another lifetime ago. The me before my daughter. The me before the marriage and divorce. The me before my mom died. Before all of it, there was a me who lived in the mountains. While I flipped through the pictures, I found myself smiling. I noticed a palpable feeling of anticipation; it felt like joy. It felt like an invitation back to myself, an invitation to do something. Because doing is the most important part.

Maybe I'll go skiing next month, or maybe I'll just take a day trip and play in the snow. Maybe I'll go find my snow gear in storage and have it ready for the next big storm. It doesn't really matter what action I take; it only matters that I do something that helps me reach past the margins of who I've become. That is how I reclaim it, own it, and then celebrate it.

This process has taken me to a piano store during the early weeks of lockdown, a few hundred miles away from my home. I booked a private hour to play every instrument in their store. I moved from bench to bench while playing Chopin, Brahms, and Bach before I found the one. It rained all the way up and all the way back home, eight hours round trip, and it was totally worth it. The piano now sits in my home.

This pursuit has taken me to my tiny kitchen floor on a winter night with my phone propped up on the countertop, a YouTube dance tutorial on its screen. My husband and I watched the moves carefully again and again before we tried to do the steps. We were willing to not take ourselves so seriously, to laugh, and to learn something new.

This pursuit has followed my love for horses and found a stable where I can volunteer. It's followed my love for painting and found a local class. It's followed my love for books, and I joined my local library's book club. Bit by bit, I find pieces of myself and do something to own them and celebrate them.

So this is where I come to reclaim myself, back to the beaches of my memories. I meet myself again and again, asking, *Who am I? What do I feel? What do I need? What do I love? What do I really want?* I walk slowly as if searching the sand for sea glass, listening for the whispered answers to arise. *I am... I feel... I need... I love... I really want...* This is where I come to find treasures that have washed up on the shore—who I was and who I've become. Some get thrown right back to the past, pieces that served me for a time but have no value in my life today. But there are others that I pick up carefully, turning them in my hand, remembering who I was then, what that felt like, and what it would mean to reclaim that part of myself again. Those are the ones I put in my pocket. Those are the ones that I line up across my desk. And then piece by piece, I do something with them.

Your worthy mind is vast, a wide-open beach with countless treasures. It wants you to walk its shores, dip your toes in the water, collect driftwood, and make sandcastles. It wants you to know that you are all of it. You are the sea glass, the shells, the stones. You are the ocean, the sky, the waves. You are every grain of sand. You are invited to walk along the shore of yourself, without argument and without defense, to say, *Yes, I am this,* again and again. You are invited to welcome home the wild little you who once played on these shores, forgive the tired battles, cherish the old scars, and embrace the hurt, the tragedy, the triumphs. To be willing to say to each and every part of you, *You belong. You are needed. Thank you.*

Life wants all of you. It wants you to gather all your knowledge, all your gifts, all your weaknesses, and all your strengths. It wants you to bring this to every relationship, every room, every conversation, and every endeavor. To reclaim your power, your strength, your tenacity—that is life changing. To rise from the ashes of your failures—that is freedom. To reclaim your faith, your hope, your joy—that is a miracle. To be able to bring your entire self and move through the world with a sense of purpose and full of ease—that is worthiness.

Reading Group Guide

1. How did it feel to acknowledge and have a conversation with your lost self? What desires and needs did you uncover during that process?

2. Which defense mechanisms do you find yourself using in your life? In what situations do you find yourself resorting to defense mechanisms? What strategies might you use to avoid using defense mechanisms in the future?

3. In Chapter 4, Meadow writes about her experience of her mother taking up the empty space that existed inside of Meadow. Have you had the experience of allowing another person to define parts of you? How did it play out for you?

4. Do you struggle to set boundaries in your relationships? How might you approach boundary setting differently after reading *The Worthy Mind*?

5. Did you participate in the Worthy Work challenges throughout the book? Which was the most difficult for you? Did you begin noticing themes in your responses?

6. Which stories from real women throughout the book did you identify with the most? If you were to include your story in the book, how might you write it?

7. Name one small way and, if you can, one large way that you will change your life after reading *The Worthy Mind*.

Notes

CHAPTER 2: HOW YOU LOST YOURSELF

1   Heather A. Berlin and Christof Koch, "Defense Mechanisms: Neuroscience Meets Psychoanalysis," *Scientific American*, April 1, 2009, https://www.scientificamerican.com/article/neuroscience-meets-psychoanalysis/.

2   Michael D. Nevarez, Melinda I. Morrill, and Robert J. Waldinger, "Thriving in Midlife: The Roles of Childhood Nurturance and Adult Defense Mechanisms," *Journal of Research in Psychology* 74, (June 2018): 35–41, https://doi.org/10.1016/j.jrp.2018.01.002.

CHAPTER 4: WHAT TOOK ITS PLACE

1   "Emotional vampire" is a term coined by psychologist Albert J. Bernstein in his book *Emotional Vampires: Dealing with People Who Drain You Dry* (New York: McGraw-Hill, 2001).

About the Author

Meadow DeVor is a self-development teacher with a modern approach to spirituality, money, and personal growth. Since 2007, she has led courses, training, and retreats both online and throughout the United States. She's the author of *Money Love: A Guide to Changing the Way You Think About Money* and has had the pleasure of being a guest on *The Oprah Winfrey Show*. She speaks, writes, and teaches extensively on how our relationship to life itself is an exact reflection of our deepest held beliefs about our own worth. She lives with her husband in Big Sur, California.

Did you love *The Worthy Mind*? Check out Meadow's online course, with even more resources to help you build self-worth!

A Daily Guide to Build Self-Worth

- Self-Care Checklists
- Confidence Affirmations
- Self-Esteem Journaling Prompts
- Self-Love Wallpaper
- Daily Activities to Help You Build Self-Worth

Here's what you'll find inside:

Self-Worth Reminders

Twelve motivational aesthetic wallpapers for your phone, tablet and laptop. If you're looking for a simple yet powerful way to stay motivated and inspired, add self-love affirmations to your daily routine with beautiful iPhone wallpapers featuring quotes to build self-worth.

Worthy Mindset Checklists

Use these checklists for assessing your self-worth and personal growth. You'll find weekly self-esteem checklists, a self-worth assessment quiz, and ways to improve low self-esteem. Find powerful mantras and self-love affirmations to help keep you in a positive mindset.

Self-Worth Activities

An ultimate guide to self-care, self-love, and building self-worth. You'll find journaling prompts, self-esteem weekly trackers, self-worth weekly planner, self-esteem worksheets for emotional triggers, self-worth daily activity list, and so much more.

Visit https://meadowdevorcourses.com/workbook-worthy -mind/ to download your free Self-Worth Workbook.